U.S. Army Uniforms
of the
Cold War

U.S. Army Uniforms of the Cold War 1948–1973

Shelby Stanton

STACKPOLE
BOOKS

Copyright © 1994 by Shelby Stanton

Published by
STACKPOLE BOOKS
5067 Ritter Road
Mechanicsburg, PA 17055

*All photographs and illustrations are from the Department
of Defense.*

Printed in the United States of America

First Edition

First paperback printing, April 1998

10 9 8 7 6 5 4 3 2

Library of Congress Cataloging-in-Publication Data

Stanton, Shelby L., 1948-
    U.S. Army uniforms of the Cold War, 1948-1973 / Shelby
Stanton. — 1st ed.
      p. cm.
    Includes bibliographical references and index.
    ISBN 0-8117-1821-2
    1. United States. Army—Uniforms—History—
20th century. 2. Cold War. I. Title.
UC483.S517   1994
355.1'4'09730904—dc20   93-13745
                                  CIP

Contents

Contents

Preface

U.S. Army Uniforms of the Cold War is the fourth volume in a series covering the development of modern Army clothing and individual equipment. This book references the Army uniforms of the Cold War that characterized the national mobilization from 1948 until the creation of a volunteer force in 1973. During this time, millions of citizens were brought into service through the peacetime draft. The uniforms of the latter Cold War period, introduced after the draft was terminated, are not treated here because they actually belong to and merge into the current Army uniform system.

This book also clarifies the continuing development and transition of Army uniform and field clothing by tracing the evolution of many military styles from their conception prior to World War II. In this capacity the book lends vital coherence to the entire series by unifying the progression of uniforms described in the other uniform books devoted to specific wars. It should be used in conjunction with the author's *U.S. Army Uniforms of World War II, U.S. Army Uniforms of the Korean War,* and *U.S. Army Uniforms of the Vietnam War* published by Stackpole Books.

During the Cold War era the Army performed extensive occupation and security missions throughout the world, and had to be clothed and equipped to fight on a global basis. The Army provided a combat presence in the Dominican Republic, the Berlin emergency, the Cuban Missile crisis, the Lebanon deployments, the Korean Demilitarized Zone defense, and other key missions, such as civil disturbance operations.

Army uniform compositions and maintenance during this period were strictly regulated and reflected the professional pride and discipline of a well-regulated citizen military. The importance of proper standards was evident in the individual soldier's living arrangements, and Appendix I is devoted to the barracks clothing and equipment inspection displays that were part of the soldier's lifestyle.

I am thankful to the many members of the U.S. Army community and National Archives staff who readily provided professional support during my research and always replied to my many inquiries for obscure historical information. Walter Bradford of the U.S. Army Center of Military History was especially helpful in reviewing the many drafts of this manuscript. Sylvia Frank and William C. Davis of Stackpole Books provided valuable editorial support. My sincerest appreciation must go to the many veterans who shared their priceless memories and private photographs, and thus truly made this book a reality.

Shelby L. Stanton
Bethesda, Maryland
1 June 1993

1

Army Uniform Employment

National Defense Considerations

During World War II the U.S. Army was clothed and equipped, for the first time in its history, to fight on a global basis. The requirement for improved uniforms and equipment continued in the postwar years, because the U.S. military was assigned to perform extensive occupation and security missions throughout the world. The ensuing Korean War expedited the provision of better weather-protective and field combat clothing assemblies. The adaptation of Army uniforms during those wars are covered in *U.S. Army Uniforms of World War II* and *U.S. Army Uniforms of the Korean War.*

The initiation of the Cold War between rival superpowers, and their allies, ushered in an era of unprecedented military preparedness and low-level conflict. The global scale of Army operations necessitated the complete revision of its clothing requirements. The lessons of Asian conflicts and European occupation had demonstrated the absolute need for soldiers to be equipped with suitable uniforms, both for short-notice deployment and prolonged presence in areas ranging from the frozen arctic to the torrid tropics. The Army uniforms adopted for the latter zone, during the Viet-

nam conflict, are covered in *U.S. Army Uniforms of the Vietnam War.*

This book focuses on the general duty and dress uniforms worn by the U.S. Army during the Cold War, when it was required to safeguard national defense, provide internal order, and respond to war-threatening emergencies. These uniforms rivaled the importance of combat attire in displaying a formidable and professional Army presence. For the public at large, garrison uniforms were the visible Army. In a very real sense, they underscored the determined resolve of the American government to meet its commitments—whether they were tested in Berlin of divided Germany, or in Little Rock of a segregated United States.

Postwar Uniform Development

At the conclusion of World War II the Army recognized the need for a better uniform for the postwar soldier. As in past conflicts, the military faced a departing veteran force and a surplus of wartime clothing items of various patterns and uneven quality, produced under emergency conditions. Also, many types of clothing and many examples of fabrics and colors had been permitted, espe-

1

New recruits step off the bus at the U.S. Army Reception Station, Fort Jackson, South Carolina, to begin processing into the military during May 1965. Each carries an "AWOL" bag, a small civilian bag containing a minimum amount of personal items.

Uniforms of the Seventh Army in Europe during 1965 include (*left to right*) food handler, parachutist, aviator, rifleman, military policeman, armored crewman, scout in overwhites for snow camouflage, artilleryman, medical specialist, and mechanic.

cially among officers, that were anything but uniform.

Prior to World War II, the Army had used its service uniform for duty in both the garrison and the field. The dress uniform, no longer issued to enlisted personnel after World War I, had been worn by officers for social occasions. Service uniform fabrics were chosen to provide appearance and comfort, as well as camouflage qualities needed on the customary battlefield. Olive drab wool serge was considered the best material for winter service in temperate-climate clay, sand, and foliage, while the summer cotton khaki twill was expected to meet the requirements of tropical campaigning.

The conditions of World War II created an entirely new set of clothing priorities. Khaki twill

2

lacked durability for jungle fighting, and olive drab herringbone twill cotton work clothing took its place as battle dress. Olive drab wood serge served well as the year-round uniform in the European theater, but by 1944, it had become part of the intermediate layer of the Army winter layering system. This was the wool uniform combined with outer shells of wind-resistant cotton in the new field jackets and trousers. [1]

Postwar uniform development was affected by the recommendations of the Doolittle Board (named for its chairman, Lt. Gen. James H. Doolittle). Established by Secretary of War Robert P. Patterson in March 1946 "to study officer-enlisted relations," this board became a forum for veteran criticism of wartime pettiness and mistreatment at the hands of the officer corps. On 19 August 1946

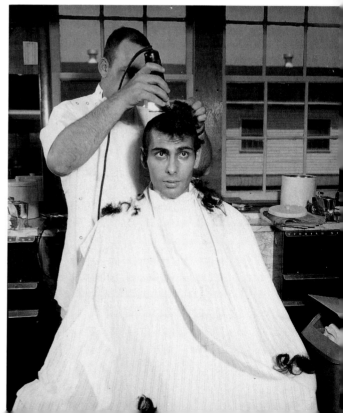

A private who has just been inducted into the Army receives the customary "G.I. haircut," given to all incoming recruits, at the U.S. Army Reception Station in Fort Knox, Kentucky, during April 1965.

New recruits in a variety of headgear (field cap, OG-106 hot-weather cap, and the OG-107 utility cap) begin learning the hand salute at the U.S. Army Reception Station, Fort Jackson, during May 1965.

New recruits, already attired in new Army underwear, receive the remainder of their initial clothing issue as part of basic processing through the U.S. Army Reception Station at Fort Jackson, during May 1965.

Newly arrived inductees are fitted for their initial issue of Army Green shade 44 uniform coats and service caps at the U.S. Army Reception Station at Fort Leonard Wood, Missouri, during April 1965.

4

the board concluded that the "military caste system" should be eliminated, and that the Army should adopt "identical uniforms for officers and enlisted personnel, except for insignia, effective 1 July 1948."[2]

To meet these requirements, the Army prescribed the wool field jacket to be the winter uniform for officers and enlisted personnel, and scheduled the elimination of various officer's uniform items and the revival of the blue uniform for all personnel. By 1948, the wool jacket was no longer designated a field garment, and a new enlisted serge equivalent of the officer's belted service coat was proposed but never implemented.[3]

The 1949 Army uniform board, the first after the war, incorporated these collective wartime experiences and postwar guidance for "leveling" uniform designs to establish the doctrine that would guide further development. Officer "pinks and greens" were still worn, but plans were undertaken to dispense with the separate officer uniform as soon as it would be practical to do so.

This Army uniform board finally resolved the service uniform dilemma of conflicting requirements. Whereas the prewar olive drab and khaki uniforms were expected to satisfy both combat and garrison conditions, the new guidance separated all uniforms into two categories: garrison and duty uniforms, and field and work clothing. This criteria restricted the need for battlefield camouflage to the latter category, and thus opened the way for a new Army color in uniform attire. The board also recognized the desirability of a separate and distinct uniform with fashionable styling for female soldiers.[4]

Army olive drab was already under criticism. As thousands of veterans returned home, their olive drab wool uniforms suffered the disgrace of becoming second-hand clothing. Government-issued olive drab clothing became cheap garments for domestic chores and shabby jobs throughout America. Laborers toiled in unkempt wool flannel shirts, weekend house painters dressed in paint-splattered wool serge trousers, and sanitation workers habitually donned soiled "Ike" field jackets. The olive drab wood serge uniform was no

Privates receive combat boots as part of their initial clothing issue at the U.S. Army Reception Station, Fort Knox, during May 1965. Their initial issue includes new-pattern hot-weather caps and 1963-pattern OG-107 fatigue shirts.

Trainees dressed in cotton sateen utility uniforms turn in blankets and bedding at the U.S. Army Reception Station, Fort Leonard Wood, in April 1965. Note white name tags on shirts.

After completing their passage through the clothing point, new recruits stand in formation beside their duffel bags, which are filled with initial clothing issue as displayed in front, at the U.S. Army Reception Station, Fort Leonard Wood, during April 1968.

longer viewed as a matter of pride, but as second-rate civilian attire.

Later scientific camouflage studies, based on wartime experience, had determined that olive green was superior to olive drab in most field settings. During the Korean War the Army produced olive green wool shirts and trousers to correspond with the olive green parkas, overcoats, trouser shells, and other components of the revised cold-wet field clothing assembly.[5]

The olive drab uniform style was also regarded as unsatisfactory for general duty, because of the disliked jacket design as well as the civilian disrepute now associated with the entire outfit. In 1954 a quartermaster uniform expert summed up its status: "And frankly there is nothing about the olive-drab shade to justify its continued use as a service uniform. The winter OD definitely has outlived its value."[6]

From Olive Drab to Army Green

The Army embarked on a major program to develop a new uniform with the sole purpose of providing proper garrison attire, thus avoiding the historical pitfalls that accompanied compromising the design to fulfill combat requirements. The same design was selected for officers and enlisted men alike, and was identical to the single-breasted, four-pocket coat styles already in place with the army white, army tan, and army blue uniforms. It

A sergeant greeting his family upon arrival from Korea wears the olive drab wool uniform that clothed the Army from the end of World War II until its transition to army green. Note the M1950 garrison cap with branch-of-service cord edge braid and crown crushed to form two peaks in characteristic G.I. style.

The changeover to the new army green uniform from 1956 to 1961 gave the soldier a modern appearance, as reflected by this 1965 recruiting poster. The uniform included matching service cap, coat, and trousers for officers and enlisted men.

Soldiers of the 6th Infantry guarding Berlin wear winter field uniforms in parade order during a review in February 1959. Field coats are combined with infantry blue scarves, M1945 combat packs, and M1936 pistol belts. The olive green wool trousers are bloused over highly polished combat boots.

was also similar to that designed by the Quartermaster Corps for the new uniform of the Air Force, which was separated from the Army in 1947.[7]

The climatic adaptability of the uniform depended on the weight and weave of its fabric, whether cotton, wool, or a blend of natural and synthetic fibers. The material also governed the uniform's intrinsic tailoring characteristics and its ability to present a sharp military appearance. The final selection ranged from winter-weight wool serge, wool elastique, or wool gabardine, in a gray-green color that became Army Green shade 44, to lightweight blended polyester/wool fabrics in a gray-green synthetic coloration named Army Green shade 344. The new colors were selected only after careful testing of textile dyes to ensure quality control and consistent color match between coat and trousers—nearly impossible in the previous military garment procurements.[8]

The proposed army green uniform was tested extensively during 1954 by soldiers of the 3d Infantry (The Old Guard), stationed at Fort Myer and Fort McNair in the national capital area, and displayed at other posts and overseas. The uniform was favorably received and, upon approval of the Army staff, the "starting gun for the Army Green uniform was finally fired in July 1954." Uniform specifications were adopted on 2 September 1954, and the Army began programming its transition as the standard Army service uniform for garrison duty, travel, and off-duty wear by all ranks.[9]

The changeover from olive drab to army green had a major impact on the uniform appearance of the citizen (drafted) soldiers and it forever served as the demarcation between the old and new Army, which served between the Korean and Vietnam conflicts. The phased transition to the new uniform seemed painfully slow, but it actually occurred in a relatively short time when the scale of the undertaking was taken into account. Factors

Military policeman of the 503d MP Bn wear winter army green uniforms with prescribed MP accouterments while guarding the Pentagon during the anti-war demonstration of 21 October 1967.

included the enormous numbers of items, the size of the Army and its worldwide dispersion, and the economical utilization of old uniforms until new garments became available.

The conversion process was carefully considered. The Department of the Army (DA) decided against simply cutting off old uniform supply and beginning the flow of new uniforms into the supply pipeline, because it would create a sudden chasm between recruits in army green and soldiers previously equipped with olive drab attire. DA also decided against changing uniforms on a geographical basis, because of the impracticality of reequipping large numbers of troops moving between areas. DA also decided against a single date for new uniform issuance, without regard for old uniform assets, because the action was unsound economically.

DA implemented a staggered schedule that attempted to make the best possible use of existing olive drab service uniforms, while ensuring the balanced distribution of the army green uniform. Residual stocks of the older uniforms were re-duced in an orderly fashion, while the "build-up" inventory of newer garments was efficiently introduced. The exact schedule and implementation details of this uniform turnover are addressed in chapters 5 and 6.

The program was initiated in November 1954, when 6 million yards of army green serge was procured and 800,000 uniforms were manufactured from this material. The program was completed by the 1960–61 period, as first projected. At its conclusion, the Army had made a total changeover from the Olive Drab shade 33 wool serge uniform, with its russet-brown accessories, to the army green uniform with black accessories.[10]

(*Right*) **The major duty of the Cold War soldier was preventing a nuclear clash between the superpowers. A 14th Armored Cavalry Regiment trooper, wearing the OG-107 field work uniform, patrols the tense Fulda Gap sector of the Iron Curtain with a German border unit during September 1963.**

(*Above*) Soldiers of the Vietnam-bound 199th Inf Bde wear summer army khaki uniforms "under arms" during activation ceremonies at Fort Benning, Georgia, on 24 June 1966. The addition of individual equipment belts, helmet liners, and bloused combat boots to the khaki uniform was typical for review purposes.

These rites of passage marked the end of the "brown shoe Army" of olive drab wool and herringbone twill. The new Army, well attired in improved army green, displayed the confidence and readiness of an authoritative military force. Army green fitted in exactly with the national policy of atomic deterrence, and complemented the U.S. desire to project the most professional soldiering image toward its Cold War adversaries.

Other Uniform Changes

The Army uniform of national mobilization during the Cold War, which lasted from 1948 until the creation of a volunteer force in 1973, was characterized by several hallmark features. Through decades of use, these uniform characteristics of the "drafted Army" acquired the accepted status of military tradition, and their ultimate replacement

Weekly inspection of a soldier's clothing was part of barracks life. During May 1964 an inspecting officer at Fort Sill, Oklahoma, checks the locker of a Specialist 4th Class for clothing condition and conformity to prescribed arrangement.

Individual equipment was displayed during a full field inspection in regulation manner, as typified by this 6th Armored Cavalry Regiment layout at Fort Meade, Maryland, during January 1968. M-14 rifle is beside the M-1956 individual field equipment.

drastically changed the countenance of the Cold War uniform.

Foremost was the two-part construction of the M1 steel helmet assembly, which allowed separation of the liner. The helmet liner could be used as lightweight headgear whenever actual battlefield protection of the heavier helmet shell was not required. The helmet liner shape, however, presented a martial facsimile for military duty, and show-of-force for ceremonial occasions. When gloss-painted and marked with insignia or distinctive trimmings, the helmet liner became a trademark of the Cold War garrison uniform.[11]

Another foundation of Army uniform attire was the continual retention of 100 percent cotton in the utility clothing "fatigue" uniforms and the standard cotton khaki uniforms. These uniforms were worn in the time-honored manner of "break starch." This practice was a cornerstone of military discipline that reflected the soldiers' pride and strict personal maintenance of their uniforms. The ideal "hard starched" crispness of cotton twill khaki, with a razor edge on the shirt and trouser creases, rendered a sharpness that symbolized Cold War garrison duty.

Equally critical as a source of military pride was the high polish that soldiers laboriously applied to uniform accessories. Hours of hand-rubbed "Brasso" polishing was mirrored in the sparkling solid-brass belt buckles, collar insignia fixtures, and cap devices that adorned the garrison and dress uniform. More hours of hand-buffing with repeated "Kiwi" wax-based shoe polish applications produced a glassy "spit-shined" finish on the russet brown (and subsequently black) leather items, shoes, and boots.

All these attributes of the Cold War uniform passed into oblivion during the Vietnam-era rush to adopt improved uniform items of civilian-inspired convenience. The trend commenced when plastic wares began replacing genuine leather articles. The drive gained momentum throughout the late 1960s, as plastic finishes began to be substituted for leather polishing.

During 1973 the Army began testing polyester cotton fabrics capable of wash-and-wear convenience. The resulting durable press shirts and trousers had the comfort and easy-cleaning attributes of civilian dress, but irrevocably compromised the khaki "break starch" tradition. The final parade-ground feature of the Cold War army was removed at the end of the decade, when the Personnel Armament System Ground Troops (PASGT) helmet replaced the M1 helmet assembly in 1978, thus eliminating the separate liner for non-combat duty.[12]

Some of the changes were made to ease maintenance burdens, some were by-products of the clothing industry's movement toward synthetics, and some were real combat improvements, such as the new helmet. Many changes, however, represented a calculated government effort to improve individual morale, by adopting as many uniform short-cuts as possible.

The total result was a relaxation of standards in military apparel, which was viewed at the time with considerable misgivings by the professional officer and non-commissioned officer (NCO) corps. The severance of the helmet liner, starched cotton, and hand-polished leather marked the passing of the drafted-citizen Army of the Cold War era. The new professional volunteer Army assumed a completely different appearance in harmony with its new identity.

1. Risch, Erna, and Thomas Pitkin, *Quartermaster Historical Series No. 16: Clothing the Soldier of World War II,* Office of the Quartermaster General, 1946.
2. WD press release, 19 August 1946.
3. WD Circular 88, 26 March 1946, and DA Circular 89, 1 April 1948.
4. DA Uniform Board Preliminary Report, 29 April 1949.
5. DA Pamphlet 355-10, 19 September 1957.
6. Lt. Col. R. T. Morgan, "Clothing Requirements," *The Quartermaster Review,* November–December 1954, p. 111.
7. OQMG, *Historical Study Series II,* No. 1, Washington, D.C., 1956.
8. Natick Laboratories, *Technical Report 68-41-CM,* March 1968.
9. Lt. Col. Reuben T. Morgan, "Clothing," *The Quartermaster Review,* November–December 1955, p. 24.
10. *Ibid,* p. 134.
11. *The Quartermaster Review,* July–August 1955, p. 56.
12. MIL-S-43929, 25 August 1975.

2

Army Blue Uniforms

Uniform Utilization

The Army's blue uniforms were descended from the traditional blue uniforms of the nineteenth century, which had been elevated to the status of dress uniforms when the olive drab service uniform was adopted in 1902. In both World Wars I and II, however, wear of the dress uniforms was prohibited for most personnel because of wartime conditions. In the postwar era the blue uniforms were authorized once again, and they were designated as winter dress commencing on 11 April 1951. The uniforms remained winter dress until 28 September 1959, when DA extended their wear to a year-round basis.[1]

The blue uniform categories were created in order to conform with the international and diplomatic protocol demanded of a first-class world power. These orders of dress also conformed to the equivalent dress uniforms of the other armed services. The four categories of army blue uniform also coincided with levels of formality in civilian attire, as follows:

1. The army blue uniform (formerly called the dress uniform), when worn with a black square-end bow tie, served as a dress uniform that corresponded to a civilian tuxedo or dinner jacket for semi-formal evening occasions.
2. The army blue uniform, when worn with a four-in-hand black necktie, served as a semi-dress uniform that conformed to the standards of a civilian business suit.
3. The blue mess uniform, an alternative uniform derived more from foreign military custom than from civilian dress, was appropriate for private formal dinners and other "black tie" social occasions.
4. The evening dress uniform, which was actually a civilian full-dress suit fitted with military appointments, conformed to civilian full evening dress (white tie or tails).

Army Blue Uniform

After the Korean War the appearance of the army blue uniform was changed to incorporate the cut and standardized features of the army tan and white uniforms. This conversion, by itself, was not detrimental, but unfortunately it was accompanied by a switch in ornamentation that dispensed with a

The army blue uniform is worn by the Army Surgeon General (*second from left*) and other senior medical officers at Camp Zama, Japan, in November 1966. The semi-dress wear of the uniform with necktie compared to the civilian business suit for social events. General officers did not wear branch-of-service insignia, but generals of the Medical Department often wore the caduceus insignia.

century of Army tradition. On 7 August 1953 the branch-of-service trouser stripes, which had existed for officers since 1851, as well as all branch trimming on the enlisted blue uniform, were changed to gold lace or gold-colored fabric.

Commencing on 1 February 1958, the army blue uniform became the prescribed uniform for attending social functions. The uniform was technically optional, but DA regulations "strongly encouraged" that it be worn for appropriate on-duty occasions and for social events after retreat. The uniform was considered clearly preferable to civilian clothes at social gatherings, both daytime and evening. Unfortunately, its purchase was a major expense, even from the post exchange at the comparatively low cost of $46.25 for the coat, $23.75 for the trousers, and $11.50 for the shoulder straps, in 1958 dollars.[2]

On 18 February 1963 DA required all officers and warrant officers to possess the army blue uniform. The uniform was also prescribed for issue to enlisted men assigned to selected organizations and the recruiting service.[3]

The army blue coat in Dark Blue shade 150 was designed with the same single-breasted, four-

pocket style already in place with the white uniform coat of 1938. The coat closed at the front with four buttons. It had semi-peaked lapels and pocket flaps pointed at the center and at each corner. The coat was made of 14-ounce wool

Berlin commander Maj. Gen. Hugh Harris wears the army blue uniform and bow tie for evening occasions. He uses a Prussian cavalry sword at a reception and staff dinner in the Berlin Officers' Club during September 1956.

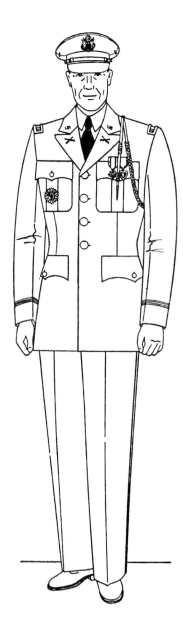

barathea, 11- or 14-ounce wool gabardine, 16-ounce wool elastique, or 10-ounce tropical wool. (The weight of material is the measurement of the fabric by the linear yard.)[4] During the 1960s blended fabrics of 9.5- to 10.5-ounce polyester/wool in either gabardine weave or tropical weave were introduced for lightweight coats for summer wear.

Officers and warrant officers wore rectangular shoulder straps sewed or snapped in a centered

(*Below*) **Sgt. Maj. of the Army George Dunaway wears the army blue uniform while greeting Gen. William Westmoreland in September 1970. Gold-colored braid trims the shoulder loop and cuff. He also wears insignia of grade and diagonal service stripes.**

(*Above*) **Army blue uniform, shown for lieutenant serving as assistant attaché with service aiguillette, Distinguished Service Cross and Purple Heart decorations, and DA General Staff Identification Badge on right pocket.**

Chief Warrant Officer Chester Heinzel wears the army blue uniform in semi-dress fashion at the Pentagon during February 1962. The warrant officer insignia is worn on the blue cap and the coat lapels, and the insignia of grade appears on the brown-and-gold shoulder straps.

Chief Warrant Officer Donald Flewell wears the army blue uniform with black bow tie at the Pentagon during June 1971. This uniform corresponded to a civilian tuxedo or semi-formal wear.

position with the long side on the shoulder head seam, and curved to fit the shoulder. The straps were bordered in gold trim, with embroidered insignia of grade on a background that was blue-black velvet for general officers, or the color of branch-of-service for other officers. A second color formed an inner border if the branch was authorized one, such as maroon field with white inner border for the Army Medical Department.

Enlisted coats had shoulder loops, piped in gold-colored braid, instead of shoulder straps. Sleeve ornamentation on the cuff consisted of gold-colored braid of various width: 1½ inches for general officers, ¼ inch on either side of a stripe in branch-of-service color for officers, and ⅛ inch for enlisted men.

The uniform was worn with a white shirt made of plain-weave cotton in commercial design, with barrel or French cuffs, and a standard turn-down collar. If the shirt had a detachable collar, a

plain white semisoft or stiff turned down collar was worn. Plain gold or gold-colored cuff links were used.

When the uniform served as evening semi-formal wear, a square-end black silk or rayon bow tie was used. On all other occasions, the uniform was worn with a black four-in-hand necktie in tropical worsted and other similar woven or knitted fabrics. The Army yielded to a popular commercial device when it authorized the optional pre-tied, snap-on necktie by DA regulations effective 5 April 1962.

The army blue trousers were Dark Blue shade 150 for general officers and Sky Blue shade 151 for all other ranks, and were made of the same material as the coat. On 10 March 1965 DA bowed to individual styling comfort by permitting the use of either low- or high-waist trousers. Gold-colored ornamentation on the outside seams consisted of two ½-inch stripes spaced a half inch apart for general officers, and one stripe 1½ inches in width for

19

Sgt. Maj. Louis of the 324th Army Material Command Band wears the army blue uniform with bow tie. The nameplate, first prescribed as black with white edging in 1956, was not required on off-duty uniforms until much later. Note Adjutant General's Corps branch-of-service insignia prescribed for wear by Army bandsmen.

other ranks. Commercial suspenders or the ordinary web waist belt could be worn underneath the coat. Footwear consisted of black leather plain-toe shoes.[5]

The blue cap was Army Blue shade 150 with a crown of fur felt or wool fabric. The cap band was blue-black velvet with gold-embroidered oak leaves for general officers, branch-of-service color silk for other officers, brown silk for warrant officers, and blue mohair for enlisted personnel, all trimmed in gold-colored braid. The chin strap for enlisted men was black leather, and for officers was brown leather covered by gold lace, rayon, or nylon. The cordovan-finish black leather visor was plain, except for field grade and higher officers (majors and above), who had dark blue (black commencing in 1959) cloth embroidered with two arcs of gold-colored oak leaves.

The blue cape was an officer accessory for the blue uniform and considered more presentable

than the overcoat. It was made of Dark Blue shade 150 barathea, gabardine, elastique, or broadcloth. The prescribed length was adjusted to cover the evening dress coat, but did not extend further than 2 inches below the knee. The blue cape lining was rayon, acetate, or synthetic satin-face cloth in dark blue for generals, brown for warrant officers, and in the first color of the branch-of-service for other officers. The taupe or later army green overcoat could be worn with the blue uniform if the blue cape was not used. On 5 November 1957 DA authorized an optional scarf of bleached white rayon, silk, or woven wool. White cotton or lisle gloves were worn as prescribed.[6]

Officers assigned as military aides wore the traditional gold-colored aiguillette. The dress aiguillette was placed on the coat for occasions calling for the black bow tie, and worn on the right shoulder by officers assigned as the military aide to the President or White House social aides (while on duty with the First Family), and by officers designated as aides to foreign heads of state. The dress aiguillette was worn on the left shoulder by officers assigned as Army attachés, assistant attachés, or other aides, and by officers regularly detailed to the Army General Staff.

The service aiguillette was worn on occasions calling for the four-in-hand necktie. It was worn on the right shoulder by officers assigned as military aides to the President or White House social aides (while on duty with the First Family) and by all officers designated as aides to foreign heads of state. The service aiguillette was worn on the left shoulder by Army personnel assigned as attachés, assistant attachés, and aides.

Officers wore, in addition to their shoulder straps, metal U.S. insignia on the collar of the coat and insignia of branch on the lapels. Enlisted insignia included metal U.S. disc insignia (right collar) and insignia of branch (left collar), including infantry discs if applicable, sleeve insignia of grade in gold color on a blue background, and gold-colored diagonal service stripes angled on the lower sleeves. Cloth shoulder sleeve insignia and tabs and organizational items, such as distinctive unit insignia and airborne background trimming (ovals), were prohibited.

Other items, such as combat and special skill badges, full-size or miniature decorations and ribbons, infantry shoulder cord, *fourragère,* General Staff Identification, Department of Defense Identification, and Joint Chiefs of Staff Identification and Presidential Service Identification commencing 1969, were worn as authorized. Depending on the occasion, full-size or miniature decorations and medals could be worn.

Blue Mess Uniform

The officers' mess uniform was a secondary uniform, first adopted in 1902. It had been influenced by the European military custom of wearing a short jacket in the officers' mess or private dining hall. Thereafter it acquired traditional Army acceptance as part of the well-dressed professional

The optional blue cape, worn with the army blue uniform, included a lining in branch-of-service color. This infantry company-grade officer has a blue cape with blue satin lining.

Aide-de-Camp Lt. Thomas Kelley wears the dress aiguillette on the left shoulder of his army blue uniform. He accompanies Maj. Gen. Edwin Carns, who is dressed in the army blue mess uniform, at an official reception at the Presidio of Monterey, California, in June 1965.

Blue mess uniforms with black cummerbunds are worn at a formal dinner party hosted by Maj. Gen. Robert Fergusson (*right*) for Australian generals at Fort Ord, California, in September 1965. Note general officer gold-colored double stripe on the trousers.

officer's complete wardrobe. The mess uniform functioned as suitably formal yet comfortable attire for the officers' club and mess, which was the center of social activities for officers and their families, and other special situations apart from enlisted troops.

The blue mess jacket was Dark Blue shade 150, and made of the same material as the army blue coat. The jacket was cut the same as an evening dress coat, but descended only to the point of the hips and was slightly curved to a peak behind and in front. Two small coat buttons, joined

by a small gold or gold-colored chain, could be worn in the upper buttonholes.[7]

The jacket lapel facings were dark blue for generals, brown for warrant officers, and in the first color of the branch-of-service for other officers. The shoulder knots were rounded at the top and formed of four plaits of triple gold bullion, gold-color nylon, or rayon cord ¼ inch in diameter, and stiffened on the underside with dark blue or black cloth.

The most traditional aspect of the blue mess jacket was the system of grade insignia incorpo-

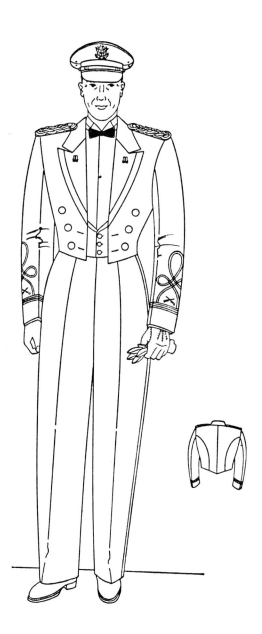

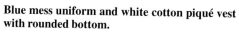

Blue mess uniform and white cotton piqué vest with rounded bottom.

Blue mess uniform and white cotton piqué vest with pointed bottom adopted in 1961.

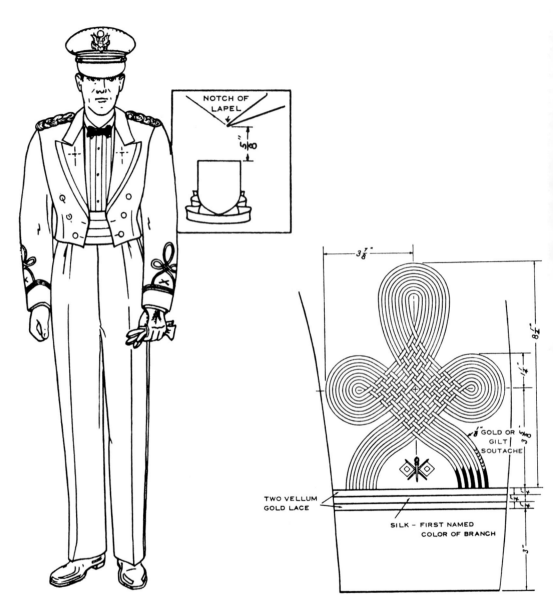

NOTCH OF LAPEL

5/8"

3 7/8"

8 1/2"

1/2"

3"

GOLD OR GILT SOUTACHE

TWO VELLUM GOLD LACE

SILK – FIRST NAMED COLOR OF BRANCH

3"

Blue mess uniform with black cummerbund, adopted in 1969, replacing vest.

Blue mess jacket cuff for colonel of Signal Corps with traditional braid in branch-of-service color. Note how braid interlaced to form a triple-looped knot.

Army blue uniforms and blue mess uniforms, along with a civilian tuxedo, are worn at a III Corps Artillery testimonial dinner at Fort Sill, Oklahoma, during March 1965. Note the early cuff ornamentation on the mess jacket (*left and center*), which featured a design that corresponded to the grade of the officer.

rated into its sleeve ornamentation. European-style multiple loops of soutache braid were adopted by the uniform regulations of 1902 for the full-dress coat, the mess jacket, and the special evening dress uniforms. This system was similar to that worn during World War I on the sleeves of the olive drab wool overcoat. With the reintroduction of dress uniforms, this form of grade insignia was retained on the mess jacket. The full-dress coat had been discontinued by 1938, and the evening dress sleeve ornamentation had been simplified in 1952.

The jacket cuff for general officers was blue-black velvet, trimmed with embroidered gold-colored oak leaves, and surmounted by starred insignia of grade. The blue mess jacket cuff for other officers had a gold-trimmed stripe in branch-of-service color, surmounted by branch-of-service insignia, and gold-colored braid interlaced to form

a triple-looped knot above the cuff that corresponded to individual grade. The knot contained five rows of braid for colonel, four rows of braid for lieutenant colonel, three rows of braid for major, two rows of braid for captain, and one row of braid for first lieutenant. The blue mess jacket sleeves for second lieutenant lacked the braided knot, and for warrant officers contained only their insignia of grade.

A white cotton piqué vest was first worn with the blue mess uniform. It had a single-breasted, low-cut pattern with rolling collar, and it fastened with three detachable small white buttons. The original rounded bottom was changed by DA regulations to a pointed bottom effective 11 January 1961.

A cummerbund was introduced as an optional alternative to the vest in January 1961. The cummerbund was preferred by the officer

Pueblo Army Depot commander Col. Louis Antol receives Legion of Merit from Ordnance Center commander Brig. Gen. David Hiester in April 1966. General officer mess jacket cuff ornamentation was velvet with embroidered oak leaves and insignia of grade.

corps, but there was some debate regarding its appropriate color. During 1963 Lt. Gen. Hamilton H. Howze and other senior officers recommended that the cummerbund be black for general officers, and in branch-of-service color for all other officers. The debate was resolved in favor of black. The vest was discontinued and the black cummerbund became mandatory effective 1 May 1969.[8]

The white semi-formal civilian dress shirt, worn with the blue mess jacket, was designed in semi-formal fashion with soft unstarched bosom, French cuffs, and an attachable or detachable turn-down collar. The shirt was worn with the square-end black evening bow tie. The studs and cuff links were plain white, such as white mother-of-pearl, with optional rims of platinum or white gold. Effective 11 January 1961 DA mandated round gold or gold-colored metal cuff links and studs instead.

The trousers were Dark Blue shade 150 for

general officers and Sky Blue shade 151 for other officers and warrant officers. The trousers were designed like civilian formal trousers, with a high waist but no cuffs or hip pockets. Trouser ornamentation matched the army blue trousers. Footwear consisted of black low-quarter shoes.

The blue cape was optional but was preferred instead of the overcoat, especially with the blue mess uniform. On 5 November 1957 DA authorized an optional scarf in bleached white rayon, silk, or woven wool, whenever the optional taupe or later army green overcoat was worn. Cotton or silk white gloves were worn as prescribed.[9]

Additional items of insignia allowed on the blue mess uniform were limited to restrict embellishments that detracted from the jacket's intrinsically abundant ornamentation. For example, insignia of grade and insignia of branch were contained within the braided sleeve design. As a result, the dress aiguillette, *fourragère,* and identification badges were allowed on the jacket, and either miniature decorations and medals or distinctive unit insignia could be displayed on the jacket lapels. All other items were prohibited.

Evening Dress Uniform

The evening dress uniform provided officers with more formality in their attire. The coat was initially a blue-black or black full-dress or formal civilian tail coat. This was converted into a military garment by replacing the civilian buttons with military ones and adding shoulder knots and sleeve ornamentation. Effective 1 May 1969 DA adopted an Army evening dress coat to replace the militarized commercial tail coat, and the latter was disallowed after 1 July 1975.[10]

The shoulder knots were the same design as those worn on the blue mess uniform. The sleeve ornamentation was simplified from the traditional coat rank system (see previous section) on 5 September 1952. The quantity of gold braid no longer varied according to grade, but consisted of a gold-colored single design with trefoil and horizontal braid on a black broadcloth background. The branch-of-service identification was replaced by insignia of grade within the design. Captain and lieutenant bars were placed parallel to the horizontal braid, instead of their normal vertical positioning, and the horizontal braid was intermittent for

The uniform board of 21 April 1972 simplified blue mess jacket ornamentation for officers, other than generals, to a gold-trimmed stripe in branch-of-service color, surmounted by insignia of grade, and one gold-colored braid interlaced to form a triple-looped knot. The previous system had multiple braids according to rank, and branch-of-service insignia instead of rank.

27

Evening dress uniform, shown for colonel, could initially be a civilian evening formal (tail) coat. Manner of wearing DA General Staff Identification Badge and Office of the Secretary of Defense Identification Badge on uniform is indicated.

Evening dress uniform, shown for lieutenant colonel, worn with riband of a foreign order. Note new-pattern trefoil cuff braid enclosing insignia of grade.

Evening dress uniform adopted in 1969, shown for major general. General officer's cuff is trimmed with embroidered oak leaves, surmounted by insignia of grade. Manner of wearing DA General Staff Identification Badge is indicated.

The 9th Army Band of U.S. Army Alaska wears the blue uniform prescribed for Army bands, with gold-colored breast cords, as it marches through downtown Sitka in October 1970. The drum major in front signals the band with his baton.

The 9th Army Band of U.S. Army Alaska performs at a change-of-flag ceremony outside Sitka in October 1970. This view shows the gold-colored shoulder knots of the army blue uniform for bands, as well as the trefoil design of the braid on the blue cap.

warrant officers. The cuff ornamentation for general officers was retained.

A white cotton piqué or other conventional civilian white evening vest was worn. The low-cut design was single-breasted with rolling collar and pointed bottom. The vest fastened with three extra-small detachable white buttons.

A full-dress formal civilian white shirt was worn with a full-dress bow necktie of plain white silk or rayon, or material matching the shirt. The shirt had a stiff bosom, such as plain starched or piqué, French cuffs, and an attached or detachable wing collar. The studs and cuff links were plain white with optional rims of platinum or white gold.

The evening dress trousers were blue-black or black and matched the material of the coat. They were patterned along the lines of civilian formal trousers without cuffs. Gold-colored ornamentation on the outside seams consisted of two ½-inch-wide stripes spaced a half inch apart for general officers, and one ¾-inch-wide stripe for other officers. Footwear consisted of black leather shoes.

The uniform included the blue cap and the blue cape, as well as dress white gloves. Only the dress aiguillette for prescribed officers was permitted on the evening dress uniform. Insignia was included in the sleeve ornamentation, and other items were limited to those displayed on the blue mess uniform.

Distinctive Blue Uniform for Army Bands and Honor Guards

Army bands had been permitted to enhance their uniforms with distinctive trimming and accessories since the nineteenth century. Nevertheless, no common Army-wide band uniform existed. To provide a standardized dress for these units, the distinctive blue uniform for Army bands and honor guards was authorized in 1956.

Components of this uniform were authorized at various times for the U.S. Army Band (Pershing's Own), the Army Ground Forces Band (redesignated the Army Field Band in 1950), U.S. Military Academy (USMA) Honor Guard, and Army-level bands. Later the 1st Battalion of the 3d Infantry (The Old Guard) and select units such as the Fort Hamilton complex ceremonial platoon

Sfc. Frank Brawner wears guards-style bearskin with gold chain chin-strap, Infantry Center Band baldric with miniature drumsticks, and white gauntlets, and holds the mace while drum major of the 291st Army Band at Fort Benning, Georgia, in October 1969.

Honor Guard of the 3d Inf (The Old Guard) wears the distinctive blue uniform for bands and honor guards at the Pentagon in July 1970. The NCO (*far left*) has guard identification badge for the Tomb of the Unknown Soldier.

were also included in this authorization. In 1969 the U.S. Army Band and Army Chorus was granted another distinctive uniform that included a scarlet cap and a coat in white or blue. The coat was fashioned in a pseudo–nineteenth-century style with stand-up collar and gold nylon shoulder cords.[11]

The distinctive blue uniform for Army bands and honor guards included an Army band blue service cap, with a Blue shade 150 crown decorated by gold-colored trefoil braid. The Army band blue coat was made of 14-ounce wool barathea in Dark Blue shade 150, except in tropical regions, where 10-ounce tropical worsted coats were furnished. A white broadcloth shirt and black mohair four-in-hand necktie were worn underneath the coat.

Gold-colored rayon Army band shoulder knots and the gold-colored detachable breast cord were placed on the coat. The Army band waist belt in Sky Blue shade 151 with the Army band belt buckle, containing the U.S. coat of arms, was fastened around the coat. The Army band blue trousers were Blue shade 151 in the same material as the coat, and featured gold lace or gold-colored ornamentation stripes sewn along the outside seams.

Musicians carried black Class 2 leather music pouches, while honor guardsmen were equipped with the Military Police (MP) black leather belt and shoulder strap. The black leather first aid packet case and .45-caliber magazine ammunition pocket were attached to the belt. Footwear consisted of black dress leather oxford shoes.

The Army band blue raincoat in AF Dark Blue shade 1157 was authorized in 1966, but issuance was confined to the U.S. Army Band and Chorus, Army Field Band, USMA Band, and the 1st Battalion, 3d Infantry (The Old Guard). The raincoat was actually a waterproof-treated dress top coat with detachable liner, made of 6-ounce nylon warp cloth and oxford rayon filling.

The Army band blue double-breasted overcoat became available in 1962, but it was restricted to the U.S. Army Band and Chorus, USMA Honor Guard, and the 1st Battalion, 3d Infantry and its associated MP company. The overcoat was made of 28-ounce wool velour twill weave in Blue shade 82. Later the Army Field Band also received permission to wear the overcoat.

The Taupe shade 79 wool gabardine overcoat was issued to regular Army-level bands, but proved unsatisfactory because it conflicted with the color of the Army band blue uniform. This situation was not resolved until 1970, when the cotton/polyester poplin raincoat in Blue shade 358 was issued to all bands and honor guards.

1. SR-600-32-1, Para. 31, 11 April 1951, and AR 670-5, Para. 29, 28 September 1959.
2. DA Circular 670-10, 19 March 1957.
3. AR 670-5, Change 13, 1 February 1958, and AR 670-5, Change 3, 18 February 1963.
4. *Dictionary of Textile Terms,* Dan River Inc., Danville, Va., 1971.
5. AR 670-5, Change 5, 10 March 1965 and AR 670-5, Change 12, 5 November 1957.
6. AR 670-5, Change 10, 29 August 1957.
7. AR 670-5, Change 1, 1 October 1969.
8. AR 670-5, Change 1, 11 January 1961, and AR 670-5, Para. 11-7, 1 May 1969, and Lt. Gen. Hamilton H. Howze ltr to Gen. Earle G. Wheeler, 10 May 1963, Tab H.
9. AR 670-5, Change 12, 5 November 1957.
10. AR 670-5, Para. 12-2, 1 May 1969.
11. DA Circular 670-8, 10 December 1956, and SB 10-573, 5 December 1962. Army-level bands listed by the circular included seven Army bands (First–Seventh) and seven U.S. Army Forces bands (Alaska, Caribbean, Europe, Pacific, Southeastern Task Force, and two in the Far East), and the Seventh Army Symphony Orchestra.

3

Army White and Distinctive Uniforms

Uniform Utilization

White uniforms were reintroduced as a part of Army attire by 1902, when permanent military forces were established in tropical territorial garrisons and overseas outposts such as the Philippines, Hawaii, and Panama. The white uniforms provided a customary degree of formality for official functions and social occasions, and were required for officers serving in tropical and semitropical regions outside the United States. The uniforms were originally made of cotton fabrics, adopted to facilitate frequent washing, but tropical worsted and other fabrics capable of dry cleaning became popular after World War II.

The white uniform corresponded to a civilian white summer suit or summer dinner-coat attire, and it served as the summer equivalent of the blue uniform. The white mess uniform was the military equivalent of the civilian white dinner jacket or tuxedo, and provided the most appropriate semiformal warm climate evening attire.

The white uniforms, however, inherently pre-sented a different degree of prestige than the winter blue uniforms, because "dress" in the summertime lacked the formality of "dress" in the winter season. Most occasions deemed necessary for the white dress were actually less formal by any standards of convention. The white uniform also failed to acquire the "dress uniform" authority implicit in the army blue uniform, because the latter constituted the traditional symbol of the U.S. Army and was an integral part of the mandatory officer wardrobe.

Disfavor toward the white uniform was based on cost and unnecessary uniform duplication, as summarized by Lt. Gen. Hamilton H. Howze in a letter to Army Chief of Staff Gen. Earle G. Wheeler on 10 May 1963:

"I believe the Army has up to now faced the dilemma of having so many, and expensive, varieties of uniform that it has not been expedient to require all officers to equip themselves completely. In any official function involving lower ranking officers, for example, one will find a vast mixture of uniforms, the mixture often including both winter and summer varieties. My recommendations [are to] minimize uniform change and hence expense, and afford considerable savings to the individual officer.

Recommendations include elimination of the white dress uniform. Although one may conjure up occasions on which such a uniform may be useful to have, it should be noted that we now habitually work in fatigues; therefore a shift to a summer dress uniform (recommended to be green instead of tan) constitutes a distinct step upward in formality of dress and hence will be suitable for informal afternoon and evening functions. The white mess jacket [alone] will do for semi-formal and formal evening functions. Civilian dress provides an additional alternative. Hence, I believe we could do without white dress and its cap."[1]

The white uniform, however, remained optional, except for officers stationed in overseas tropics, where its longstanding requisite status was retained. The uniform was not mandated elsewhere, but officers returning from tropical regions

Army white uniforms are worn at Fort McNair in Washington, D.C., during June 1961. The white uniform was the preferred optional dress for summer formalities in the D.C. area, but its wear was atypical at most stateside posts.

The army white uniform was considered the equivalent military attire of the business suit. Note how the dark suit of Secretary of the Army Stephen Ailes contrasts unfavorably with the white uniforms, which were intended to harmonize with the lighter shades of summer civilian suits.

frequently wore it at their new duty stations. DA "strongly encouraged" officers, warrant officers, and enlisted men past 21 May 1957 to acquire the white uniform for appropriate semi-formal hot-weather occasions, but this requirement was entirely optional.[2]

Perhaps one of the most important influences of the army white uniform was its impact on the postwar line of other Army service and dress uniforms. The coat design adopted in 1938 reintroduced a beltless, semi-fitted style that presented a neater image than the fitted waist and flaring skirt of the olive drab service coat. Furthermore, the coat had a consistent style of pocket flaps that avoided the olive drab uniform coat's contrasting pocket types. These design features, first utilized in the army white coat, became the basis for the wartime tropical worsted semi-dress coat, and the postwar modern army green uniform.

Army White Uniform

The white cap was made of white cotton twill (or duck before 1959) or optional tropical worsted and gabardine fabrics. The cap band was plain white braid, trimmed at the bottom in dark blue cloth, which was changed to black in 1959. The chin straps for enlisted men were black, and for officers were brown covered by gold-colored lace, rayon, or nylon. The visor was cordovan-finish black leather. For field grade and higher officers the visor was topped with dark blue cloth, or black cloth commencing in 1959, embroidered with two arcs of gold-colored oak leaves.

The single-breasted army white coat was made of 8.2-ounce white cotton twill (alternate cotton duck until 1959), 10-ounce tropical worsted, or 11-ounce wool gabardine. After 1960 the coat was also manufactured of 9-ounce polyester/wool blended fabrics in tropical weave or 8-ounce polyester/viscose blended fabrics in gabardine weave.[3]

The coat design included semi-peaked lapels, shoulder loops, and four pockets with flaps pointed at the ends and center. Officer coat ornamentation consisted of a ½-inch white cotton or mohair braid around the cuffs. Enlisted men were authorized a thin stripe of gold-colored braid around the lower sleeve from 1 May 1969 until the order was rescinded on 1 October. White cotton or lisle gloves were worn as prescribed.[4]

The white shirt was made of plain-weave cotton in commercial design, with barrel or French cuffs, and standard turndown collar. When the shirt had a detachable collar, a plain white semisoft or stiff turn-down collar was worn. The cuff links were plain gold or gold-colored metal.

The uniform could be worn with a square-end black silk or rayon evening dress bow tie, which converted it to evening dress standards. On all other occasions the uniform was worn with a black four-in-hand necktie in tropical worsted or similar woven fabric, or knitted fabric commencing in 1963. An optional pre-tied, snap-on necktie was permitted by DA regulations effective 5 April 1962.

Commercial suspenders or a waist belt could be worn underneath the coat. The army white trousers, made of the same material as the coat, were of standard design without pleats or cuffs, and contained watch, hip, and side pockets. The trousers were worn with black leather plain-toe shoes.

The dress aiguillette was placed on the coat by prescribed personnel when it was worn with black bow tie. The service aiguillette was used when the coat was worn with necktie. Officers wore U.S. insignia on the collars of the coat, insignia of branch on the lapels, and insignia of grade on the shoulder loops. Enlisted men wore U.S. insignia on the right collar and insignia of

Army COFS Creighton Abrams decorates Sgt. Maj. of the Army Silas Copeland at Fort Myer, Virginia, in June 1973. Copeland wears enlisted army white uniform with gold-colored insignia of rank and service stripes. The gold braid around the cuff was authorized for enlisted coats during 1969 only.

Commanding General of the Military District of Washington, Maj. Gen. Curtis Herrick, wears the army white cap in September 1966. The black visor was embroidered with gold-colored arc of oak leaves, prescribed for field-grade officers and above.

Army white uniforms are worn in semi-dress fashion to a reception honoring the Army representatives of the American republics in May 1961. The uniform was mandatory for officers serving in tropical regions outside the United States.

branch on the left collar of the coat, with infantry discs if applicable, insignia of grade on a white background (matching coat) on the sleeves, distinctive items authorized for infantrymen, and gold-colored nylon or rayon diagonal service stripes angled on the lower sleeves. Other items of decorations were worn as permitted on the blue uniform.

White Mess Uniform

The white mess jacket was also made of 8.2-ounce white cotton twill (or duck until 1959), 10-ounce tropical worsted, or 11-ounce wool gabardine. After 1960 it was also manufactured of 9-ounce polyester/wool in tropical weave or 10.5-ounce polyester/wool in gabardine weave for more comfortable summer fitting.

Maj. Gen. Clarke Baldwin Jr. wears the army white uniform during promotion ceremonies at the Pentagon in August 1971. The uniform was optional in the United States, but was the preferred attire for official functions and social events in southern regions.

White mess uniform and white cotton piqué vest with rounded bottom, as worn before 1961.

The white mess uniform was considered the most appropriate attire for formal evening dinners and social functions of an official nature during the summer season, and included a white mess jacket with shoulder knots, black bow tie, and black trousers.

Army white uniform, shown for master sergeant, with shoulder loops piped in gold-colored braid and embroidered insignia of grade and diagonal service stripes on each sleeve.

The jacket was cut the same as an evening dress coat, but descended only to the point of the hips and was slightly curved to a peak behind and in front. Two small coat buttons, joined by a small gold or gold-colored chain, could be worn in the upper buttonholes. The shoulder knots were the same design as those worn on the blue mess uniform. The jacket sleeve ornamentation was the same as on the blue mess jacket, except that the braid was white (see chapter 2).

The mess white vest was made of the same material as the coat in 11-ounce weight or less, or with cotton piqué. The vest had a single-breasted, low-cut style with rolling collar that fastened with three detachable extra-small white buttons. The vest contained a rounded bottom, without points, until 11 January 1961, when DA regulations prescribed a pointed bottom instead. A black cummerbund could be worn instead of the vest.[5]

The black dress trousers were made of lightweight material, with a high waist design and no hip pockets, and had a black silk or satin stripe along the seams. On 5 April 1962 DA authorized trousers to be fashioned with or without pleats. Other uniform items, except the white cap, were the same as the blue mess uniform.[6]

Distinctive Old Guard Uniforms

Elements of the 3d Infantry (The Old Guard), stationed at Fort Myer outside Washington, D.C., were accorded distinctive uniforms for ceremonial purposes, military functions, and special honors within the capital area. The distinctive blue uniform for Army bands and honor guards (see chapter 2) constituted the primary attire for duties like guarding the Tomb of the Unknown Soldier. Several other uniforms, based on historical examples, contributed to the military formality of high-level receptions, and were more directly connected with the unit's status as the nation's oldest regular infantry regiment.

The Old Guard Fife and Drum Corps was created during 1959–60 as part of the 3d Infantry. The uniform was based on that worn by regimental musicians in 1784, when the regiment was first formed. The Fife and Drum Corps wore a black military cocked hat with white binding and the alliance white-and-black cockade with a white wig. The regimental coats of red, faced blue, were worn

The Continental Color Guard of the 3d Infantry (The Old Guard) performs honors at the Mount Vernon historical estate of George Washington in 1970. The guardsmen carry (*left to right*) the national color, Army flag, and regimental color.

The Old Guard Fife and Drum Corps of the 3d Infantry provides a full honor ceremony for the departure of a foreign dignitary from the White House in January 1970. Note spontoon held in lowered salute position by drum major (*left*) at gate entrance.

This view of the Old Guard Fife and Drum Corps shows how the coat skirts were hooked back for marching during a full honor arrival ceremony at the White House during 1970. Note bugles and rope-tension "Soistman drum" (*left*).

with white waistcoats, britches, stockings, and black buckled shoes, which are actually military low-quarter shoes with laced-in brass buckles. Corps instruments consisted of bugles, fifes, and rope-tension "Soistman drums" emblazoned with the 3d Infantry coat of arms, which included the shield of the United States—a distinct privilege.[7]

The drum major of the Fife and Drum Corps wore a fur-crested light infantry cap encircled by a turban. He used an officer's spontoon to give commands to the Corps. His baldric, worn as a shoulder belt symbol of office, was reminiscent of the carriage used to support eighteenth-century field drums. The rest of the drum major's uniform matched that of the Corps musicians.

The Continental Color Guard of the 3d Infantry was long a traditional feature of the regiment. It carried not only the national and organizational colors, but also the flag of the U.S. Army, which was adopted in 1956.

By 1960 the distinctive uniform of the Continental Color Guard was a version of the 1784 regimental uniform. It was composed of the black cocked hat with white binding and alliance cockade and white wig, regimental line coat of blue with red facings, white waistcoat, and white overalls that fitted over the shoes with straps under the instep. Armed members of the Guard carried reproduction wood canteens and a 1763-model Charleville musket.

During 1973 the 3d Infantry expanded its Continental-era Army interpretation to provide the President with a traditional escort. Company A was redesignated as the Commander in Chief's Guard. The uniforms were identical to the Continental Color Guard, except that officers carried the spontoon as a symbol of rank and wore a sword on a shoulder belt. Enlisted troops wore crossed shoulder belts supporting a cartridge box and bayonet scabbard.

1. Lt. Gen. Hamilton H. Howze ltr to Gen. Earle G. Wheeler, 10 May 1963, p. 1 and Tab C.
2. AR 670-5, Change 8, 21 May 1957.
3. AR 670-5, Para. 70, 28 September 1959, and AR 670-5, Para. 8-4, 23 September 1966.
4. AR 670-5, Para. 8-5, 1 May 1969, and AR 670-5, Change 1, 1 October 1969.
5. AR 670-5, Change 1, 11 January 1961.
6. AR 670-5, Change 2, 5 April 1962.
7. The drums, known as "Soistman drums," were manufactured by Charles J. Soistman Jr. of Baltimore, Maryland, who started making colonial-style drums in 1959.

4

Officers' Olive Drab Winter Semi-Dress Uniform

Uniform Utilization

The olive drab semi-dress uniform was worn exclusively by Army officers and warrant officers. The uniform was informally known as the "pinks and greens" because of the contrasting scheme between the coat of Olive Drab shade 51 (dark green) and the trousers of Olive Drab shade 54 ("pinks").

The uniform had gradually evolved from the British influence of World War I as the officers' winter service uniform. During the inter-war period several fabric weaves of different shades had been authorized for officers' uniforms, and an increasing contrast developed between the shades. The difference originated with the shade-matching difficulties for any uniform ensemble, but also reflected the need for a different fabric to construct quality breeches (*i.e.,* elastique or cavalry twill) for riding fit and serviceability. In 1941 the shade was stabilized and thousands of officers wore this uniform during World War II, thus establishing it as the "pinks and greens."

The "pinks and greens" uniform ceased to be the officers' winter service uniform following the recommendations of the 1946 Doolittle Board that officers and enlisted men dress alike. In 1948 the uniform was limited to semi-dress status for officer assignments and duties while not in formation with troops. The uniform was worn at routine official and off-post social functions, and during off-duty hours after retreat (normally after 5 P.M.). Officers could use either the "pinks and greens" or the optional army blue uniform for more formal social events.[1]

The uniform's distinct appearance and established officer appearance also made it acceptable as a "dress uniform for special occasions or duties." This special permission was extended for officers attending designated formal official or social functions, or while serving as an aide to a high official or person of prominent social status. This was usually reserved for such events as official or social White House functions, or while in the company of a chief executive of another country, reigning royal family members, cabinet members, or other dignitaries.

During 1957 DA required officers to acquire the army green uniform and restricted the "pinks

Constabulary Forces commander Maj. Gen. Ernest Harmon (*right*) wears Olive Drab shade 51 wool coat, khaki cotton-mohair necktie, Olive Drab shade 54 elastique breeches, and legging-top boots in Germany during May 1946.

and greens" to off-duty wear. At that time, officers were required to own either the army blue uniform or "pinks or greens," but not both. On 1 February 1958 the army blue uniform became the prescribed uniform for attending social functions and the "pinks and greens" were no longer permitted, except that National Guard and Reserve officers were permitted to wear them until 1 October 1959. Effective 11 January 1961 DA deleted it from uniform regulations, and a major era in Army uniforms came to an end.[2]

Officers and warrant officers of the Fuchu Ordnance Depot (8123d Army Unit) in Japan wear "pinks and greens" service uniforms with Olive Drab shade 51 neckties during November 1953.

Maj. Gen. Thomas Herren wears the semi-dress winter "pinks and greens" uniform in Frankfurt, Germany, during October 1954. Note the optional commercial rain cover over his service cap.

Officers' winter olive drab semi-dress "pinks and greens" uniform (*left*) compared to the army tan (khaki tropical worsted "TWs") worn as summer semi-dress uniform. (Insignia have been deleted on these illustrations for clarity of view.)

Army surgeons wear olive drab wool coats and the short serge jacket (*left*) with the brown felt service cap and wool garrison cap on Okinawa in February 1955. Note the British-style buckle on the cloth belt of a tailor-made uniform (*center*).

Uniform Components

Several variations of the uniform developed during World War II were worn in the post-war period. The more popular version was introduced as the M1944 coat and trousers. The single-breasted four-pocket coat was made of 14- to 19-ounce wool, elastique, or barathea in Olive Drab shade 51. It had shoulder loops, peaked lapels, and a buttoned front with three regulation coat buttons and one lower plastic button. The main distinction of this garment was its construction with a fitted waist made possible by a horizontal waist seam. The last button was covered by the coat's self-material belt, supported by two belt loops set into the side seams. The gold-colored metal (GCM) belt buckle had a raised line-pattern design with rounded corner. Earlier types had a smooth rectangular rim. The belt end passed through the buckle

to the left, and was secured by a cloth keeper. Commissioned officers were indicated by ½-inch-wide Olive Drab shade 53 braid around the cuff. Warrant officers did not wear this braid.[3]

A khaki or tan cotton shirt was worn with this coat. The 1949-pattern 4-ounce Khaki shade 1 poplin shirt, made of broadcloth or dacron/cotton material, was specifically designed to be worn under a uniform coat or jacket. This shirt had a stand-up collar, no shoulder loops, a left breast pocket, and one-button cuffs. Other optional military-style khaki shirts, made of other fabrics, were permitted.

The Olive Drab shade 54 wool trousers were made of the same material as the coat and were designed without pleats or cuffs. The M1944 design introduced wide belt loops and, like most other officer garments, had buttoned flaps on the rear pockets.

The "pinks and green" uniform worn by Army COFS Gen. Maxwell Taylor (*second from left*) and supply management officers at Fort Lee, Virginia, in December 1955. Note the wear of the overseas service bars, nicknamed "Hershey bars," on the right cuff.

The Olive Drab shade 51 elastique coat with the prescribed rounded lined-surface buckle (*right*) is contrasted to an earlier rectangular version buckle at Camp Gary, San Marcos, Texas, in December 1956. Note swagger stick with two stars.

Maj. Gen. Thomas deShazo and his aide, Captain Nist, greet Portuguese general at Fort Sill, Oklahoma, during November 1956. The dual-tone "pinks and greens" dark coat and lighter trousers contrast with the solid color uniform combination.

Uniform Accessories

The service cap for officers resulted from a need for suitable headgear that could be worn with both the "pinks and greens" and the olive drab wool serge uniforms. Originally this cap had a dark olive drab wool elastique crown that matched the winter semi-dress coat, wire grommet, and a leather chin strap of ¾-inch width.

The new service cap, produced under specifications dated 29 May 1951, had a crown of fur felt in Brown shade 62, and a soft roll grommet. A band of basket-weave braid in Olive Drab shade 53 encircled the cap, which had a leather visor (slanted 45 degrees) in Russet shade 90, with a matching ⅝-inch-wide chin strap and head strap.[4]

The Olive Drab shade 51 (dark green) wool garrison cap was designed in standard fashion with a curtain containing cord-edge braid in gold for generals, gold intermixed with black for commissioned officers, and silver intermixed with black for warrant officers. The garrison cap was worn in travel status and when prescribed by unit commanders, especially when the shirt replaced the coat as the outer garment.

A commercial olive drab sweater was allowed underneath the coat. Russet leather gloves were worn whenever the overcoat was worn, or as directed. White gloves could be worn on ceremonial occasions when prescribed by commanding officers.

The World War II–era cotton-mohair necktie

CONARC CG Gen. Willard Wyman wears russet gloves with the "pinks and greens" uniform while visiting the 1st Inf Div at Fort Riley, Kansas, in February 1957. Officers around him wear brown felt service caps with raised chin straps and head straps around back.

The semi-dress "pinks and greens" are worn by officers in direct contrast to wool serge duty uniforms of other personnel, despite postwar policy requiring officers and enlisted men to wear the same uniforms. Trousers are bloused into jump boots, a recognized privilege of airborne units. 11th Abn Div, Germany, October 1956.

Transportation Col. James Higgins wears the Olive Drab shade 51 elastique coat and Brown fur felt shade 62 service cap with older-pattern ¾-inch chin strap in March 1952. DA regulations reduced the width of the chin strap during the same year.

in Khaki shade 5 was worn until 1948, when the mohair-cotton necktie in Olive Drab shade 51 (dark green) was mandated. On 1 May 1957 officers were required to switch to the black four-in-hand necktie in tropical worsted or other similar woven fabrics.

Commercial suspenders could be worn and a waist belt was required only when the coat was removed. Olive drab, olive green, or khaki web belts with plain solid brass buckles were worn.[5]

Footwear consisted of russet low-quarter service shoes or plain-toe blucher oxford-pattern shoes until 1 September 1956, when black low-quarter shoes were mandated. Black leather shoes of commercial plain toe, blucher oxford, or similar design were also permitted.

1. WD Circular 88, 26 March 1946, and DA Circular 89, 1 April 1948.
2. AR 670-5, Para. 38, 28 September 1959, and AR 670-5, Change 1, 11 January 1961.
3. PQD 149, 14 March 1942, and PQD 149C, 4 March 1944.
4. MIL-C-1687A, 29 May 1951.
5. AR 670-5, Change 10, 29 August 1957.

5

Olive Drab Winter Duty Uniform

Uniform Utilization

The wool serge uniform of the early Cold War era was known as the "OD" (pronounced as O-D) uniform not only because it was produced in olive drab, but also to distinguish it from the summer uniform of khaki. Furthermore, the uniform color was designated as Olive Drab shade 33 to differentiate it from the darker Olive Drab shade 51 worn by officer personnel in their semi-dress uniform.

The olive drab uniform was worn by all ranks as the Army winter general duty uniform, and served as the normal seasonal attire for formations. It had originated during World War II to fill the need for an adequate winter field uniform for operations in northern Europe. The main feature of this uniform was its distinctive "Ike" jacket, by which title most civilians called the attire. General of the Army Dwight D. Eisenhower, who was influenced by British battle dress, had worn his own custom-tailored version of this waist-length jacket, and this uniform forever bore his name.

The olive drab uniform was originally de-signed to provide dual-function practicality in both garrison and field situations. By the postwar era it ceased being used for field duty because the tailored jacket was uncomfortable underneath the M1943 cotton field jacket. Soldiers preferred wool shirts and sweaters instead, and saved their wool serge jackets for wear on overnight and weekend pass.

The uniform design initiated a tremendous influence in American women's and teenage fashion, and permanently altered the look of police and other public service uniforms, but it failed to satisfy the demands of a completely acceptable Army uniform. The hip-length "Ike" jacket complemented the stature of taller servicemen, but further stunted the appearance of short or stocky soldiers. It also tended to rise above the waist constantly, especially when the wearer extended his arms, stood up, or merely shifted position. This motion exposed the rumpled shirt underneath and resulted in an untidy appearance. This was especially evident with the postwar styling that called for a higher waist and a snug fit.

First sergeant of the 1st and technical sergeant of the 9th Inf Div during ceremonies in France in August 1946 wear the Olive Drab shade 33 wool serge field jacket and trousers. Khaki shade 5 mohair ties were worn until 1948, when the Army began switching to Olive Drab shade 51 neckties.

To prevent the constant tugging of jackets in order to straighten the uniform, soldiers and many units (especially those stationed in Europe and Japan) purchased and installed hooks and eyes to secure the jacket to the trousers or to the trouser web waist belt. One veteran recalled the devices as "small but made of a high-strength wire and almost unbreakable. Once they were hooked, they stayed hooked." The attachments were placed about 3½ to 4 inches from the front buttons on each garment. "Once the company tailor figured out how high the hook should be, it was sewn onto small tabs of cloth so they could be easily adjusted

The Olive Drab shade 33 wool serge field jacket and trousers served as the winter service uniform for officers and enlisted soldiers alike, as shown by this infantry guard formation welcoming King Haakon VII back to postwar Norway. Note the wear of the olive drab wool shirt with the wool field jacket.

The olive drab wool serge jacket and trousers worn by a 7797th Army Unit (Signal Depot Group) honor guard at Hanau, Germany, in April 1950. Lt. William Shulte (*left*) wears MP russet leather belt and shoulder strap, while soldiers have web M1923 cartridge belts. Note the long-waist feature of the 1944-pattern wool field jacket worn by the general inspecting the troops.

[within the jacket] if needed. It always took a couple of fittings to get the things right." [1]

The olive drab uniform was phased out during a program of transition to the army green uniform. Originally servicemen had been issued two sets of the uniform as part of their initial allowance. Commencing on 1 July 1957, a "one-and-one" issue procedure began that changed the soldier's initial allowance to one olive drab uniform and one army green uniform. Beyond that date, officers were restricted from wearing the olive drab uniform unless in formation. The uniform remained authorized for general duty wear, however, by enlisted men and for military formations.[2]

The "one-and-one" issue date marked the beginning of the wear-out period for the olive drab uniform, which was programmed to remain in the supply system until stocks were reduced to the point that further supply was uneconomical. This point was reached on 30 September 1958, and the soldier's initial allowance was switched entirely to army green uniforms.

In the meantime, until 30 September 1958, the olive drab uniform remained authorized as a general duty winter uniform and enlisted men were required to maintain at least one set. Soldiers who entered the Army prior to the "one-and-one" issue, and thus owned only olive drab uniforms, discarded their old uniforms as they became unserviceable and purchased army green uniforms using their cash maintenance allowances.

Throughout the transition period enlisted men were attired in different uniforms, and this included troop formations. DA restricted unit commanders from ordering soldiers in formation to wear just one type of uniform, except during unit formations for ceremonial purposes. In such cases, all troops wore olive drab uniforms before 1 October 1958, and only wore army green uniforms in ceremonial formations afterward.

Further officer wear of the olive drab uniform

Corp. John Graves wears the Olive Drab shade 33 wool jacket, tailored to the shorter waist of the 1947 pattern, at Fort Sill, Oklahoma, in April 1951. The "double set" of brass insignia worn on the collar and lapel was authorized from 1946 until 1951.

Soldiers of the 4th Inf Div arrive at Bremerhaven, Germany, in May 1951, wearing HBT cotton fatigue clothing and carrying pressed olive drab wool serge uniforms hooked on their regulation M1945 combat and cargo field pack assemblies. Note the pocket flaps of the wool serge field trousers on the train inspector (*right*).

was disallowed in 1959. The transition period for enlisted men continued until 1 October 1960. Wearing the olive drab uniform was prohibited past that date. The olive drab wool serge uniform was declared officially obsolete effective 11 January 1961, and the olive drab color, a feature of uniforms since 1902, passed into history.[3]

Uniform Components

The uniform jacket passed through an evolution of cut that reflected its changing function. Any or all of these versions remained in use long after they had been superseded by DA, especially among senior NCOs and older officers.

The 1944-pattern olive drab wool field jacket ("Ike" jacket) was made of 14- to 19-ounce wool serge in Olive Drab shade 33. The jacket design was single-breasted with convertible collar and lapel features, and included shoulder loops, two upper box-pleated pockets with snap-fastened flaps, and buttoned cuffs. The concealed-button front closure was fastened with four olive drab plastic buttons. A waistband was sewn around the bottom of the jacket, and it contained side buckle adjustments and a button-and-snap fastened closure on the waistband tab extension. The jacket

Sgt. Lawrence Hogsed, under arms for troop movement, wears the M1950 wool serge jacket while boarding a train in Ulm, Germany, during August 1956. He has M1 rifle, dismounted M1923 .30-caliber cartridge belt, and M1942 first aid packet pouch.

had intentionally been designed as a long-waisted garment for field practicality. The waistband could be worn low on the hip for warmth, or raised to normal position, which gave a bloused effect for ease of movement.

After World War II the MQ1 olive drab wool jacket was produced in response to the postwar desire for neater garrison uniforms. It was adopted in 1947 and produced under specifications approved on 7 June 1948. The MQ1 version was shorter and better tailored, because the service jacket no longer required the loose fit necessary for a field garment. Many of the earlier jackets were altered in conformity with the new design, and form-fitting was often accomplished. The later version of the Olive Drab shade 33 wool serge jacket was a redesign of earlier patterns and had a button-tab waistband instead of side buckles.

The M1950 olive drab wool jacket, produced according to specifications adopted in 1951, was a further refinement of the original design. The buttoned cuffs were replaced by straight coat-style

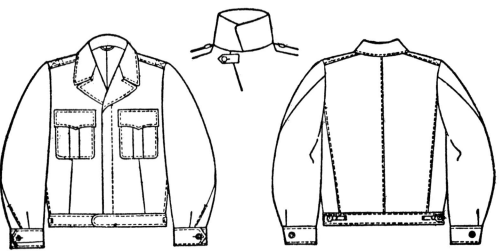

1944-pattern olive drab wool field jacket.

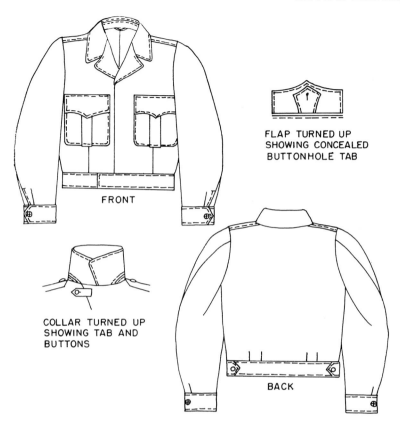

FLAP TURNED UP
SHOWING CONCEALED
BUTTONHOLE TAB

FRONT

COLLAR TURNED UP
SHOWING TAB AND
BUTTONS

BACK

MQ1 olive drab wool jacket.

sleeves, the side button-tab waistband was revised, and the back was bloused to provide greater flexibility when bending or stretching. The jacket was also given a closer fit and shortened to the soldier's natural waistline, directly over the trouser belt.[4]

The jacket was generally worn with a Khaki shade 1 cotton shirt with stand-up collar, which was made of either 8.2-ounce twill or 6-ounce poplin. The M1949 poplin shirt had a stand-up collar, no shoulder loops, a left breast pocket, and one-button cuffs.[5]

The wool serge uniform trousers were changed from light Olive Drab shade 32 to match the jacket. Both the M1952 Olive Drab shade 33 wool serge trousers and Olive Drab shade 33 18-ounce wool serge trousers were designed with two straight side pockets, a right front watch pocket on the waistband seam, and a button or slide-fastened fly. A characteristic of the original use of these

garments as field trousers was the feature of hip pockets closed with a tab-and-button flap.

The older olive drab uniforms were retained for the U.S. Army Constabulary in occupied Germany, Military Police, pack artillery units, and ceremonial troops of the Berlin Command. The wool service breeches were worn with legging-top boots in a fashion that devolved from the uniforms for mounted troops. The supply of these articles stopped effective 13 May 1955, and authorization ceased with the introduction of the army green uniform.[6]

Uniform Accessories

The service cap for officers was fur felt in Army Brown shade 62 with the soft roll grommet (described in chapter 4). The service cap for enlisted men was reintroduced in a new form in 1946. One

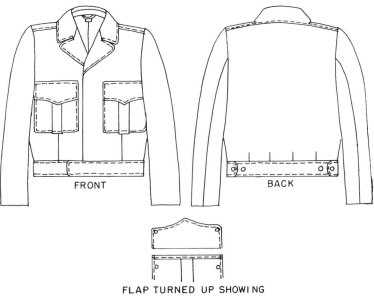

FRONT   BACK

FLAP TURNED UP SHOWING
SNAP FASTENER
POSITIONS

M1950 olive drab wool jacket.

cap frame was issued, along with two covers to match seasonal uniforms: cotton khaki for summer and wool serge in Olive Drab shade 33 for winter. The cap frame consisted of an olive drab fabric band with a leather Russet shade 90 visor and matching ¾-inch chin strap.[7]

The appearance of the enlisted service cap was altered by the introduction of a roll grommet. Soldiers often altered this grommet to reconfigure the cap's former stiff "flying saucer" silhouette into popular but unauthorized styles, such as the curved "Mexican bow" or "saddle" shape. This practice was tolerated in many units, and its widespread acceptance even allowed these modish caps to become characteristic of honor units and Military Police.

Sgt. Paul Guiterez of the 322d Signal Bn in Darmstadt, Germany, wears the Olive Drab shade 33 wool serge jacket with non-issue domed collar insignia during 1953. Soldiers were able to "peak" the M1950 garrison cap by crushing the center portion of its crown, a practice prohibited in 1956.

Brig. Gen. Joseph Harper, 4th Inf Div commander, wears the M1950 olive drab wool serge
jacket at Frankfurt, Germany, in April 1953.
He has combat leaders' "green tab" identification on the shoulder loops, from which hangs
the French *fourragère* and Netherlands Orange
Lanyard.

Officers wear an issue Olive Drab shade 33
wool jacket with service cap (*left*) and a tailored
wool jacket with garrison cap (*right*) at Trois
Fontaine Ordnance Depot in August 1952. The
custom model featured a wide waistband.

The postwar Army uniform concept planned
for the service cap to be the only headgear for the
duty uniform, thus eliminating the garrison cap.
Between 1951 and 1954, however, the service cap
was dropped from the initial clothing allowance
for enlisted men as a result of the Korean War,
when the garrison cap alone was issued. When the
service cap was brought back into the supply system, further plans to eradicate the garrison cap
were canceled and both caps remained part of the
uniform system.[8]

The M1950 garrison cap was of standard curtain design without a gusset along the center seam.
It was worn in travel status and when prescribed
by unit commanders, especially when the shirt was
worn instead of the jacket as an outer garment.
During times of mobilization, the service cap was

not issued because of cost and inconvenience, and
the garrison cap served instead as the principal
headgear.

The garrison cap was made of matching
Olive Drab shade 33 wool serge fabric and had
cord-edge braid along its upturned curtain. This
braid was in the branch color of the assigned unit
for enlisted men, and was gold for generals, gold
intermixed with black for commissioned officers,
and silver intermixed with black for warrant
officers.

A rayon scarf in branch-of-service color
could be worn beneath the jacket for ceremonial
purposes. Russet or black leather gloves were
worn for certain formations or as directed. White
gloves could be worn during prescribed ceremonial occasions.

The Khaki shade 5 cotton-mohair necktie,

Members of the 709th MP Bn wear olive drab wool serge uniforms with MP accessories in Frankfurt, Germany, in October 1949. Note brassards, service cap white chin straps, white pistol lanyards, and MP leather belts with holster, magazine pocket, and first aid pouch.

adopted in 1943, was worn until the Army first changed to the necktie in Olive Drab shade 51 (dark green) in 1948. By the time the black necktie became mandatory, on 1 January 1958 for troop formations, the olive drab wool serge uniform was being phased out. When local regulations permitted the shirt as an outer garment (with jacket removed), the necktie was tucked between the second and third buttons.[9]

Commercial suspenders could be worn underneath the coat, and a waist belt was required only when the shirt replaced the coat as the outer garment. The Olive Drab shade 3 web belt with GCM buckle was authorized after 1948. The olive green or khaki web belts were optional. After 29 August 1957 officers who wore a belt were required to wear a black web or woven elastic belt.[10]

Tan low-quarter service shoes or russet combat service boots were worn until 1 September 1956, when black footwear was mandated. Throughout the transition period many servicemen used dark brown shoe polish that darkened the leather, leading to a 1955 DA directive, "Commanders will direct their attention to the color of footwear during regular inspections to insure the practice of improperly dyeing leather is discontinued."[11]

The appearance of the olive drab uniform varied with command, and those of the separate 6th Infantry Regiment in Berlin during the mid-1950s was one example. One former officer remembered:

"This was the standard OD uniform of the period. Almost everyone had them well tailored because tailoring was free in the company and inexpensive from such excellent uniform tailors as Fritsch and Rohr on Kurfurs-

Maj. James Fowler of the 366th Infantry in December 1949 wears a flight jacket in dark olive drab elastique. Developed by the Army Air Forces as an equivalent to the "Ike" jacket, it was one of several jackets that became obsolete in 1948. Note brown fur felt service cap with pre-1936 pattern cap insignia.

Troops of the 287th MP Horse Platoon, Berlin Command, wear olive drab wool serge jackets with elastique service breeches during May 1956. Authorization for the mounted uniform ceased with the introduction of the army green uniform.

tendamm. Tailoring often included sewing down the pockets, the lapels, and the shoulder loops and stiffening the waistband and making it the exact width of a pistol belt. Some had hooks set in the lower edge that would hold the pistol belt exactly in place in spite of any movement. These jackets could not be worn without the pistol belt so they became parade jackets. The pistol belt was dyed black and almost all of its grommets filled with bolted-in brass semi-hemispheres we called studs. These and the two brass slides on the belt were highly shined. The blue branch-of-service scarves were worn, and there was considerable disagreement whether wearing a shirt with it was necessary, desirable, or messed up the hang of the jacket. The parade helmet liner was enameled a high gloss black with the Berlin Command insignia centered in front and the 6th Infantry Regiment insignia on the sides. As the last was mostly white and red, it stood out nicely."[12]

1. Bill Berebitsky, correspondence to author, 31 December 1992.
2. DA Circular 670-14, 8 May 1957.
3. AR 670-5, Para. 45, 20 September 1956; AR 670-5, Para. 38, 28 September 1959; AR 670-5, Change 1, 11 January 1961.
4. MIL-J-10801
5. DA Circular 4, 7 January 1953.
6. DA Circular 725-8400-1, 13 May 1955.
7. USA 8-151, USA 9-101, and USA 20-185, 22 August 1947.
8. SR 32-20-2, 21 December 1951 and 16 June 1954.
9. DA Circular 670-14, 8 May 1957.
10. AR 670-5, Change 10, 29 August 1957, and QMCTC-3, 9 February 1949.
11. DA Circular 670-2, 17 May 1955, and DA Circular 670-5, 10 July 1956.
12. Scot Crerar, correspondence to author, 3 June 1992.

6

Army Green Uniform

Uniform Utilization

The army green uniform was developed to replace the officer olive drab semi-dress ("pinks and greens") as well as the general duty olive drab wool serge uniform, and so provide one winter garrison and duty uniform for all ranks. In this capacity, the uniform would also provide seasonal travel and off-duty attire for all servicemen. When suitable lightweight fabrics later became available, the army green uniform was approved for year-round wear. This began the end of seasonal uniform changes.

On 2 September 1954, following considerable development, the army green uniform was adopted. DA established a prolonged transition period to allow an orderly changeover in attire as other uniforms were withdrawn from the system, and to ensure availability of the new uniform through regular supply channels (see chapter 1). On 1 May 1957 the army green uniform became available for officer purchase from the Army–Air Force exchange service and quartermaster clothing sales at a cost of $65.75.

On 1 July 1957 the Army commenced a "one-and-one" issue procedure for the initial clothing allowance of two service uniforms per each enlisted soldier. One was the army green uniform and the other was still the olive drab uniform. Effective the same date, enlisted men were given the option of wearing either the army green uniform or the olive drab uniform for general duty during the upcoming winter season. The army green uniform also became available from both commercial sources and quartermaster sales outlets, and became mandatory for officers on 1 October 1957.[1]

Throughout the transition to the new uniform, many enlisted men were attired in either army green or olive drab uniforms, and this mixture included troop formations. DA expected and allowed for temporary wearing of different uniforms within the same units, as long as items were not interchanged with other uniforms. During the transition period, commanders were prohibited from ordering soldiers to appear in just one type of uniform during formations, unless they were ceremonial events.

On 1 October 1958 the army green uniform became the standard winter duty uniform for all occasions. The soldier's initial allowance was now upgraded to two sets of army green uniforms and accessories. Further issuance of the olive drab uniform was stopped, and all servicemen were required to own at least one army green uniform.

The army green uniform became the winter duty uniform on 1 October 1958. Lt. Quentin Richardson wears the officer black mohair cuff braid and gold chin strap. Note the distinctive infantry blue shoulder cord.

Soldiers who still lacked the army green uniform secured the apparel with cash maintenance allowances. Finally, on 1 October 1960, the uniform became the mandatory winter service uniform attire for all Army servicemen.[2]

Most high-ranking officers favored upgrading the army green uniform's material content and year-round adaptability, as Lt. Gen. Hamilton H. Howze wrote to Army Chief of Staff Gen. Earle G. Wheeler on 10 May 1963:

"A very tight rein should be kept on quality control. Quartermaster outlets and post exchanges are both guilty of selling shoddy-appearing uniforms. The issue enlisted green uniform is soft and fuzzy, and so are many uniforms found on officers. All cloth should be of the hard variety, capable of accepting and keeping a sharp press. Taking the lead from the Air Force [blue uniform], a summer weight army green uniform should be provided to replace the present TW coat and trousers."[3]

The cost efficiency and convenience of adopting the army green uniform for all seasons was reinforced by the success of optional officer uniforms, made of quality lightweight fabrics. The concept of making summertime army green service uniforms for enlisted personnel gained momentum. DA began earnestly investigating material suitable for mass production that could be used for this purpose. During 1961 several fabrics were selected and underwent stringent uniform testing.

On 28 October 1963 DA certified two manufacturers to produce a 9.5-ounce lightweight blended cloth, consisting of 40 percent wool and 60 percent polyester fiber in a tropical weave. The program led to the adoption of specifications for a lightweight army green uniform on 13 July 1964. This uniform was authorized for year-round wear by all ranks, effective 10 March 1965.[4]

On 1 July 1965 the lightweight uniform became available for optional purchase through the Army clothing sales stores, but only 50,000 sets

The army green winter uniform (*right*) of Army Medical Service Corps chief Col. William Hamrick is contrasted to the army tan summer uniform (*left*) of Col. Herman Jones at Fort Riley, Kansas, in October 1965. Note common army green uniform accessories worn with both uniforms.

were available by that date, necessitating storage at selected sites. In order to assure maximum availability to active army personnel, sales of the new uniform to reservists and national guardsmen were suspended until the following summer.[5]

After this date the army green uniform became the uniform for both winter and summer

throughout the Army. The uniform was also authorized as a "dress uniform for special occasions or duties." This special permission was extended while attending designated formal official or social functions, or while serving as an aide to a high official or person of prominent social status. This was usually reserved for such events as official or

The easy fit of postwar uniform tailoring, as seen in this photograph, depended on natural wool fabrics to give the uniform a sharp military aspect. Unfortunately, this classic draping of the uniform was not reproduced when lightweight blend fabrics, of 11-ounce weight or less, were worn. As a result, officers were asked to pose for their official photographs in heavier weight uniforms to ensure a superior appearance.

Sp4 Jerry Allgood receives the Silver Star at Fort Dix, New Jersey, during March 1969. His army green uniform has infantry distinctions of shoulder cord and plastic discs behind cap and collar insignia.

A sergeant wears army green uniform in "standard dress for military funerals" with chrome-plated helmet, white shoulder cord, and old-pattern equipment in white coloration (M1956 pistol belt, M7 bayonet scabbard, and M1942 first aid packet case) at Fort Benjamin Harrison in March 1966.

social White House functions, or while in the company of a chief executive of another country, reigning royal family members, and cabinet members. The blue uniform, however, usually filled this function.

Starting on 1 October 1969, enlisted men were authorized to wear the army green uniform with the white shirt and black bow tie at formal social occasions. This uniform category gave enlisted personnel an issue alternative to the army blue uniform.[6]

The army green uniform was also worn in several specialized modes, some of which are illustrated in this book. The common foundation for upgrading the basic uniform in such fashion was the individual equipment belt, or web pistol belt. Depending on the function, the belt either designated special status during formations and reviews or performed its intended role. Whenever the individual equipment belt was worn with the coat, its interlocking buckle was positioned over the shank of the lower coat button, so that the button was still visible.

The army green uniform "under arms" stemmed from the longstanding military tradition of having soldiers attired for ceremonial purposes in their service uniforms, along with appropriate cartridge or ammunition belts and weapons. The unwieldy bulk of the universal small arms ammunition cases, however, encouraged their detachment, so that the plain belt became symbolic of the entire individual equipment system. Thus, during ceremonial formations, the belt signified that the soldier was "under arms," even if a weapon was not carried and the ammunition cases were absent.

The army green uniform "under arms" was also employed as a sign of recognition. For example, in training centers the cadre wore helmet liners with the individual equipment belt, while drill instructors wore the service, or "campaign," hat with the belt. Although prohibited by policy, it was not unheard of for drill sergeants to employ the belt in corporal fashion to enforce discipline

A 339th Engineer Bn detail wears the army green uniform equipped for military funerals at Fort Lewis, Washington, in March 1967. The pallbearers wear white service caps while the firing party has white helmet liners. Red scarves are worn.

among unruly trainees. The trainees were only allowed to dress in the same fashion as a tribute of soldiering recognition during graduation exercises.

The army green uniform for honor guards and the standard dress for military funerals added individual equipment belts or white web pistol belts, with accessories typified by helmet liners, colored scarves, white gloves, and distinctive trimmings such as special shoulder cords. Weapons were carried in accordance with assigned positions by appropriate personnel.

The army green duty uniform equipped for domestic disturbances was employed for situations involving civil unrest and for show-of-force operations outside the United States, such as in Berlin or Korea. The individual equipment belt was worn with attached small arms ammunition cases, canteen, and first aid field dressing case. This gear was worn in conjunction with helmets or helmet liners and protective masks and carriers. Man-packed radios and other necessary combat or medical gear, as well as weapons, were carried by all authorized personnel.

The Sharpe Army Depot Color Guard wears army green uniforms with chrome-plated helmets, white scarves, gloves, and adjustable web color sling and belts at Lathrop, California, during April 1970. Note decorative pattern formed by the white boot laces.

Sp4 Wayne LeMasters wears the army green uniform with new traffic safety ensemble at the Pentagon in February 1963. The lighted red baton was carried and reflective green-and-white cross straps and sleeves were worn with standard MP accessories for night duty.

Additions to uniform for Officer Candidate School are worn on the (*left to right*) army green uniform, khaki uniform, and utility uniform by Signal Corps students at Fort Gordon, Georgia, in October 1965. Gold-colored metal "OCS" block letters are displayed on both collars.

Capt. Theodore Fischer and his training company wear army green uniform under arms with individual equipment belts and helmet liners upon graduation at the Fort Lewis Army Training Center, Washington, in September 1966. Note drill sergeant in service hat (*far right*).

(*Above*) MPs wearing army green uniforms equipped for domestic disturbances, with PRC-25 radios and other gear, are directed by Asst COFS for Operations, Brig. Gen. Samuel Koster (*right*), atop the Pentagon during the 27 October 1967 anti-war demonstration.

(*Right*) The army green uniform equipped for domestic disturbances is worn by Lt. Col. Thomas Adair, 503d MP Bn and Pentagon defensive commander, while securing the Pentagon during the anti-war demonstration on 21 October 1967. Note his binocular case.

(*Left*) Composite honor guard of the Berlin Brigade in army green uniforms under arms is inspected by Gen. Paul Freeman Jr. in February 1965. Note general officers' belt and gold-plated buckle of Brig. Gen. John Hay (*center*), commander of the Berlin Brigade.

Soldiers wearing army green uniforms equipped for domestic disturbances are positioned at the Pentagon during the night of the 21 October 1967 anti-war demonstration. Note helmet liners, M1956 individual equipment, and M1949 black leather gloves.

MPs, wearing the army green duty uniform equipped for domestic disturbances, poise their M14 rifles at high port while guarding the Pentagon against anti-war protesters on 21 October 1967. Note the fixed M6 bayonets sheathed in M8A1 scabbards, individual equipment belts, and M17 ABC field protective mask carriers.

Differences between enlisted and officer army green uniforms are depicted as Brig. Gen. William Glasgow decorates Sgt. Maj. Phillip Moore at Fort Belvoir, Virginia, in October 1967. General officer trousers are trimmed with two ½-inch-wide black mohair stripes.

Uniform Components

The army green uniform coat was designed with the same single-breasted, four-pocket style already in place with the white uniform coat of 1938 and the khaki semi-dress coat adopted in 1942. The coat had semi-peaked lapels and shoulder loops, and buttoned down the front with four large regulation buttons. The outside pocket flaps were pointed in the center and on each corner.

Coat ornamentation for commissioned officers and warrant officers included a ¾-inch braid of black mohair around each cuff, except that the braid for general officers was 1½ inches wide. This was a major change in the width of the braid that had existed since before World War I for designated commissioned officers. The width was changed in accordance with Army postwar policy that reduced the equivalent trimming on women's uniforms. The ½-inch braid of black ribbed mohair was reserved for female officer coats.

The army green uniform coat in Army Green shade 44 was a winter weight coat made of wool serge, wool elastique, or wool gabardine. The first material used was 14- to 18-ounce wool serge, but 16-ounce wool elastique (initially optional for officers) was adopted for the coat in 1959. Finally, on 11 January 1961, an 11-ounce wool gabardine was announced for coat production, along with another wool serge in 12-ounce weight.[7]

The lightweight army green uniform coat in Army Green shade 344 was made of blended polyester/wool fabrics. These were originally optional for officers, but later approved for regular coat manufacture. On 5 April 1962 the 10-ounce blended wool/polyester gabardine weave was specified. On 12 October 1963 the 9-ounce polyester/wool in tropical weave became the second

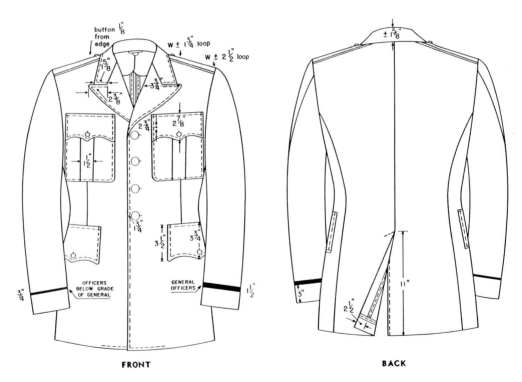

FRONT **BACK**

Army green uniform coat, showing variation in width for officers' sleeve braid. Enlisted coats lacked sleeve braid ornamentation.

Army green uniform of typical senior NCOs, in this case of the 555th Engineer Group at Karlsruhe, Germany, during September 1968, highlight tailoring details and insignia. Note embroidered Pathfinder badge on lower sleeve (*right*).

blend fabric selected. The lightweight army green uniform was adopted for enlisted issue on 13 July 1964, but not added to the clothing allowance until 1966.[8]

Several different shirts could be worn with the army green uniform. The Tan shade 46 shirt, made of 3.5- to 4-ounce cotton poplin, was adopted by QMCTC 3-55 and specifically de-

signed to harmonize with Army Green shade 44 used in the army green uniform. The tan coloration was slightly lighter than the Khaki shade 1 cotton poplin shirt, which substituted until the newer tan shirt became available in late 1957. Both shirts had a stand-up collar, no shoulder loops, a left breast pocket, and one-button cuffs.[9]

The Tan shade 446 shirt, made of 2.8- to 3.2-

Army green uniforms worn by generals and sergeants-major at Fort McNair in October 1970 show the fit of the four-button coat that permits the skirt to fly open.

Upper detail of the enlisted army green uniform coat, as worn by Medal of Honor recipient Sp5 Charles Hagemeister, just prior to decoration ceremony during 1968. Note placement of enlisted collar insignia with the vertical axis aligned with the inside edge of the collar.

The officers' army green uniform coat, as worn by Lt. Harry French, has U.S. insignia on collar and the branch-of-service insignia on lapels. The 3d Inf distinctive unit insignia is the buff strap (black-and-buff leather strap) worn on left shoulder.

ounce weight polyester and cotton broadcloth, was authorized by DA regulations on 10 March 1965. The new tan shade reflected the color difference that occurred when cotton polyester fabric was used. This shirt was also made out of 4-ounce cotton poplin or broadcloth.[10]

Other optional khaki or tan shirts, designed in the same military style and made of nylon and similar synthetic fabrics, could be worn with the uniform, except in formation with troops. A white shirt of plain weave cotton, synthetic or blend cloth, could be worn with the black bow tie by enlisted men on social occasions effective 1 October 1969.[11]

The army green uniform trousers were made of the same material as the coat. The trousers had a standard design, without pleats or cuffs, and contained two straight side pockets, two hip pockets with buttoned tabs, a right front watch pocket, and slide-fastened fly closure. Officers had a black mohair stripe 1½ inches wide down the outside trouser seams. Generals had two ½-inch stripes.[12]

Breeches in winter weight wool Army Green shade 44, or lightweight blended polyester/wool in tropical weave Army Green shade 344, were produced for wear with black leather, legging-top boots and cavalry-style steel chrome-plated spurs by the Army Caisson Platoon of the 3d Infantry.

Uniform Accessories

The army green uniform had matching headgear, usually made of the same fabric as the coat and trousers. For officers the army green service cap was also available in fur felt in Army Green shade 244, such as the better "Luxenberg" commercial brand. The enlisted service cap was issued in wool serge Army Green shade 44.

Chin straps of the army green service cap are worn in the manner traditionally reserved for mounted units by NCOs of the 2d Bn, 13th Artillery at Fort Sill, Oklahoma, in 1961. The black leather chin strap consisted of two parts, each with one end forming a slide and the other fastened to the cap by a small side button.

The 2d Bn, 13th Artillery sergeant-major (*left*) and Battery A 1st Sgt. Paul Weideman (*right*) wear service caps with hard grommets, which can be compared to the soft grommet of the service cap of Lt. Col. Hugh Martin Jr. at Fort Sill during April 1961.

The fit and appearance of the army green uniform, worn with either the garrison or service cap, is displayed by 22d Signal Group senior NCOs at Mannheim, Germany, during 1968.

The service cap had a hard roll grommet, no head strap, and a plain black leather visor with a shell cordovan finish. The service caps for field grade officers (major and above) were furnished with a black fabric-covered visor having two arcs of gold bullion oak leaves. Officer service caps had a light brown pigskin or sheepskin ⅝-inch-wide chin strap covered with two-vellum gold wire lace, and enlisted caps had a black leather chin strap.

The quality appearance of officer-model caps, however, was frequently eroded by tarnishing of the gold-colored embroidery and strap coverings. This condition was often aggravated by contact with sulfurous materials through improper

handling and storage, and by the use of plastic rain covers. The effect of this corrosion process was a dirty green patina, actually favored by some "crusty" field grade officers.

The garrison cap was made of wool serge in Army Green shade 44. Optional fabrics in different weights were also authorized for officer uniforms. The issue garrison cap for enlisted men was designed with a stiffened interfacing to keep its shape, which prevented the soldiers from peaking their caps by crushing the center portion of the crown—a traditional practice that had been disallowed in 1956.

The garrison cap had a new, straighter curtain design that diminished the curvature of earlier versions. The cord edge braid was gold for generals, gold intermixed with black for commissioned officers, and silver intermixed with black for warrant officers. The traditional system of branch colors on the enlisted garrison cap was eliminated, and the cord edge braid was prescribed in non-contrasting Army Green shade 45.[13]

The service hat was worn by drill sergeants, and the green beret was worn by Army Special Forces, as explained in chapter 7. A rayon bib-type scarf in branch-of-service color was permitted under the coat collar, covering the neck opening, for ceremonial purposes. Black leather gloves were worn in formation as directed, and white gloves could be worn on ceremonial occasions.

A judicial robe, of the type customarily worn in the U.S. Court of Military Appeals, was authorized for officers designated as military judges

Comparison between the army green uniform with service cap of Army Sgt. Maj. Silas Copeland (*right*) and M1965 field coat and service hat of Drill Sergeant Sfc. Samuel Nesbitt (*left*) at Fort Jackson, South Carolina, in January 1971.

Drill sergeants were entitled to wear their army green uniforms with the olive drab felt service hat, as shown at Fort Lewis, Washington, in April 1971. Note the Thunderer whistle and chain on left shoulder.

and appellate military judges, when participating in trials by court-martial or hearings by a Court of Military Review and during other judicial proceedings. This practice was first mentioned in regulations of 1 May 1969.[14]

The uniform necktie was a black four-in-hand necktie in tropical worsted or other similar woven fabrics. Commencing in 1963 the necktie could also be made of knitted fabric. An optional pre-tied, snap-on necktie was permitted by DA regulations effective 5 April 1962. When local regulations permitted removing the coat, the necktie was tucked between the second and third buttons of the shirt.

For added warmth, a commercial olive drab sweater could be worn underneath the coat. Commercial suspenders could be worn underneath the coat in a unexposed fashion, but a waist belt was

required when the coat was removed.

The waist belt was the Olive Drab shade 3 web belt with GCM buckle. On 29 August 1957 officers were directed to switch to a black web or optional woven-elastic belt. Effective 13 June 1958 enlisted men were authorized to wear the black web waist belt, except in formation. On 1 October 1958 this belt became part of initial clothing issues for soldiers, and on 15 April 1959 it officially replaced the olive drab belt.[15]

The trousers were worn with black military low-quarter shoes or bloused into black combat service boots. Commercial black leather shoes in plain toe, blucher oxford, chukka boot, or similar design were allowed. Commercial synthetic (cor-fram) material with leather finish was permitted on optional footwear commencing in 1969, but patent leather finishes were forbidden.[16]

1. DA Circular 670-12, 2 May 1957; DA Circular 670-14, 8 May 1957; and "AAFEX Report," *The Quartermaster Review,* March–April 1957, p. 65.
2. AR 670-5, Para. 22, 24, 28 September 1959.
3. Lt. Gen. Hamilton H. Howze ltr to Gen. Earle G. Wheeler, 10 May 1963, Tab A.
4. AR 670-5, Change 5, 10 March 1965.
5. Office of the Deputy Chief of Staff for Logistics, *Annual Historical Summary for Fiscal Year 1965.*
6. AR 670-5, Change 1, 1 October 1969.
7. AR 670-5, Change 1, 11 January 1961.
8. AR 670-5, Change 2, 5 April 1962; AR 670-5, Change 4, 12 October 1963; and AR 700-8400-1, Change 15, 20 May 1956.
9. AR 670-5, 28 September 1959.
10. AR 670-5, Change 5, 10 March 1965.
11. AR 670-5, Change 1, 1 October 1969.
12. MIL-C-13990 and M-T-13982.
13. AR 670-5, Change 4, 31 January 1957, and DA DCSPER radio message, 26 March 1956.
14. AR 670-5, Para. 4-9, 1 May 1969.
15. AR 670-5, Change 10, 29 August 1957, and DA Circular 670-27, 13 June 1958.
16. AR 670-5, Change 1, 1 October 1969.

7

Army Tan (Tropical Worsted) Uniform

Uniform Utilization

The khaki tropical worsted (TW) uniform, later re-designated as the army tan uniform, was worn by officers and warrant officers as an alternative to the cotton khaki uniform and as a summer duty or semi-dress uniform. It was optional for enlisted men but, as a practical matter, was usually restricted to NCO purchase. During the summertime the uniform with coat was the one usually worn by officers, warrant officers, and senior sergeants for official duty and social functions, as well as for seasonal social events after retreat.

The tropical worsted uniform originated with better quality fabrics worn by officers in place of the cotton service uniform before World War II. The cotton coat had been phased out, and to respond to the need for a semi-dress uniform, a new beltless coat was adopted in 1942 for officer wear. This uniform was named after the lightweight wool weave made with worsted yarns, called tropical worsted, that was used to manufacture "Palm Beach" civilian suits.[1]

This uniform was also produced from wool gabardines and other summer suiting fabrics. On 28 September 1959 the Army regulations simplified uniform terminology, and the tropical worsted uniform was redesignated as the army tan uniform. Despite this official change, the familiar term "TW" persisted within the Army ranks.[2]

The military distinction between colors, such as tan and khaki, reflected the fact that exact coloration changed with weave and fiber composition. Thus, the Army term "tan" referred to the color of tropical worsted or equivalent suiting material, as opposed to the color of khaki cotton twill, which the Army deemed to be true khaki. From this perspective it is possible to understand how the Army could call tropical worsted fabric a tan color, when it is actually a khaki hue by artistic definition.

By 1946 the Army designated Tan shade 61 to differentiate optional officer-quality khaki tropical material from standard-issue khaki cotton twill. Thus, from its inception Tan shade 61 (originally known as Khaki shade 61) was reserved for

Maj. Laurence D. Gay of the Pentagon staff communications office wears the khaki tropical worsted coat and service cap stiffened by flat grommet during May 1949. The armored force branch-of-service insignia is worn on coat lapels.

Soft roll grommet service cap is worn with the khaki tropical worsted jacket by Col. John Hayes at Fort McClellan, Alabama, during May 1953. Note Chemical Corps branch-of-service insignia on jacket lapels.

the khaki tint of tropical worsted and its equivalent summer fabrics. A variety of other fabric colors covered a wide spectrum that ranged from the cooler "silver khaki," adopted by the Air Force, through the warmer variants. Furthermore, DA introduced a new tan shade during the 1960s by adopting an orange-cast shade, gleaned from the U.S. Marine Corps, which was designated Tan shade M-1.

Officer and NCO preference for this better quality lightweight fabric continued with the wearing of the optional tan uniform, with coat removed, as a substitute for the standard khaki cotton uniform. Its tailoring and ease of care made the tan uniform popular, and the expense of purchase and dry-cleaning enhanced its prestige.

The conformity between tan and khaki uniforms was maintained, and DA mandated short-sleeve tan shirts after short-sleeve khaki shirts were introduced with conventional trousers. The army tan uniform (without coat) was authorized

for continued wear after the full coat version was declared obsolete. Since this uniform was not issued, except to special personnel, such as drill sergeants, it clashed noticeably with conventional army khaki uniforms if different sets were worn in close ranks. DA responded with regulations that prohibited wearing tan uniforms in formation by enlisted personnel.

The army tan uniform with coat not only served as the officers' Class A summer duty and semi-dress uniform, but also was habitually employed as a summer dress uniform in lieu of the army white uniform. This practice was accepted on and around military posts because all officers possessed the uniform, whereas the white uniform was optional unless the officer was stationed in the tropics.

The tan uniform with coat was even permitted to be worn in the capacity of a summer "dress uniform for special occasions or duties." This special permission was reserved for attendance at high ceremonies or special events, like White House functions, or while in the company of eminent officials such as the President, Vice President, a chief executive of another country, reigning royal family members, or cabinet members.

While permitted, the Army's use of the tan uniform as "dress" attire was somewhat limited in social occasions, especially when compared with the required white uniforms of the Navy and Marine Corps. Fashion precepts gave brown color the connotation of merely practical dress on the level of "town and country" suits. By its nature, the army tan uniform was a duty uniform and implied the lack of special expense that was required when purchasing the immaculate white dress reserved for formal occasions.

The inherent social criticism of the army tan uniform was alleviated by the 1959 DA designation of the blue uniform as the proper dress uniform on a year-round basis. During the same year the same-style army green uniform became the winter uniform and, coupled with the army tan uniform for summer wear, achieved Army design consistency for both seasons. In addition, army green uniform accessories were introduced as part of the army tan uniform.

The advent of lightweight green uniforms ultimately dispensed with the need for the separate army tan uniform for summertime wear. By the mid-1960s the complete army tan uniform with coat acquired an increasingly antiquated appearance as more officers and NCOs switched to the army green uniform for duty wear throughout the year.

The complete army tan uniform with coat was already out of military fashion by 10 March 1965, when DA announced pending obsolescence, and it became obsolete on 31 December 1968. With the demise of the Class A summer uniform consisting of long-sleeve shirt worn with a necktie, the resulting summer tan uniform then became short-sleeve shirt and trousers. It continued to serve as a popular officer and NCO alternative to the standard khaki cotton summer uniform.[3]

In February 1968 Army Chief of Staff Gen. Harold K. Johnson ordered the expeditious development of a summer duty uniform treated for durable press. He insisted on maintaining the Army tradition of seven military creases in the shirt, a hallmark of the tan summer uniform. Development was difficult because industrial state-

The khaki tropical worsted uniform coat, worn by Lt. Harold Hartstein at Fort McNair in July 1952, has 3d Inf distinctive unit insignia of buff strap on left shoulder. Note decoration and service ribbons mounted on cloth background matching the coat, which was detachable for cleaning.

of-the-art production techniques were incapable of applying the multiple sharp creases and meeting the close shade expectations of the military.

U.S. Army Natick Laboratories undertook a production engineering program that developed new techniques to apply the creases to the shirt. In addition, this high-priority program corrected the most critical problems of shade control and retention of durable press characteristics in the fabric. An ensuing Natick engineering test by six hundred drill sergeants resulted in good acceptability and established the suitability of the new clothing. Approval for optional uniform purchase was recommended.

On 29 September 1969 DA relaxed shading standards, which granted more color fluctuation and allowed optional purchasing of the shirt-and-trouser combinations: "Uniforms being offered for sale by the Army–Air Force exchange system are

Army tan uniform worn as summer semi-dress during a reception after awards ceremony at Fort McPherson, Georgia, during June 1965. The captain (*right*), aide-de-camp to the general, has gold-colored service aiguillette on left shoulder.

within the temporarily acceptable shade tolerance range as established by the U.S. Army Uniform Quality Control Officer, and therefore are approved for wear by Army personnel."[4]

Finally, in March 1970, the durable-press army tan uniform was approved for optional purchase on an Army-wide basis. The durable-press shirt and trousers were made of 6.6-ounce poly-ester/rayon blended fabrics in tropical weave, colored Tan shade 445. Production problems continued to generate color-matching problems between shirt and trousers. The easy-maintenance garments became the new basis of the tan uniform, and its popularity ensured the demise of the standard army khaki cotton uniform, which wrinkled badly unless it was starched and pressed.[5]

Uniform Components

The tropical worsted summer uniform coat in Tan shade 61 was designated the army tan uniform coat in 1959. It was designed with the same single-breasted, four-pocket style already in place with the white uniform coat of 1938, and used in the first tropical worsted coats of 1942. The coat had semi-peaked lapels and shoulder loops, and buttoned down the front with four large regulation buttons. Outside pocket flaps were pointed in the center and at each corner. Officer coat ornamentation included a ½-inch braid of Khaki shade 5 around each cuff.

The trousers worn with either the coat or the shirt-version army tan or tropical worsted uniforms matched the garment in material content, color, and weight. The trousers were usually made of 10-ounce tropical wool or similar lightweight material. The design was standard, without pleats or cuffs, and contained two side pockets, two hip pockets with buttoned flaps, a watch pocket, and slide-fastened fly closure.

Several different shirts could be worn with the army tan coat. The 4-ounce Khaki shade 1 cotton poplin shirt was adopted by QMCTC 1-50 and established the basic design of one left breast pocket, a stand-up collar, no shoulder loops, and one-button cuffs. The shirt was also produced in broadcloth and other material. On 18 October 1955 a variant style of this khaki shirt, having a two-piece quilted stand-up collar, was approved.

A new model shirt was adopted by QMCTC 3-55 for wear with the new army green uniform coat. This Tan shade 46 shirt was also approved for wear with the army tan uniform and became readily available during 1957. It was made of 4-ounce cotton poplin in a design similar to the khaki poplin shirt. This same shirt pattern was later produced in polyester/cotton fabrics as the Tan shade 446 shirt. Other optional military-style khaki or tan shirts, made of synthetic fabrics like nylon, could be worn except in formation with troops.[6]

Another class of shirts was specifically designed to be worn without the coat. These shirts were designed identically with the long-sleeve khaki cotton uniform shirt, but made of better quality and lighter material.

The style of these shirts owed a great deal to the high-quality garments of the prewar Army and the design of the officers' shirt of 1924. The wear-

The army tan uniform worn by Brig. Gen. John Hayes, senior logistics advisor to the Republic of Korea Army, in August 1964. The customized dual-language nameplate has English and Hangul characters, designed to facilitate counterpart working relationships.

ing, since that time, of a tailored tropical worsted shirt with its sharply pressed military creases had been the mark of a professional military man. This tradition was continued with the Khaki or Tan shade 61 shirt and later Tan shade M-1 shirt. Each had a stand-up collar designed to be worn with a necktie and shoulder loops. The two breast pockets could have either rectangular or clip-cornered flaps, and the cuffs could be either single or double buttoned. Both tan shirts were made of 9.5- or 10.5-ounce tropical wool, 11-ounce wool gabardine, 9-ounce polyester/wool blended fabrics in tropical weave, and 10.5-ounce polyester/wool blended fabrics in gabardine weave.

The army tan uniforms are worn with army green service caps and black neckties by Maj. Julius Golder and Lt. Col. George Price Jr. during a review at Fort Lewis, Washington, in May 1967. The uniform with coat became obsolete in 1968.

Lt. James Grooms of the Armed Forces Special Weapons Project Intelligence Division during 1948 wears the Khaki shade 1 tropical worsted service cap and shirt with the Khaki shade 5 cotton/mohair necktie, which was worn by officers from 1942 until 1948. Note the military intelligence reserve branch-of-service insignia.

U.S. Army Pacific CG Gen. Bruce Clarke wears the khaki tropical worsted shirt with the Olive Drab shade 51 necktie in Hawaii during July 1955. The Class A summer uniform with necktie and service cap contrasts sharply to the HBT field uniform with burlap-covered helmet.

A short sleeve Tan shade 61 shirt was authorized effective 3 September 1959 for wear with tan trousers, and it retained the stand-up collar of the long-sleeve shirt. These shirts had a collar lining of smooth fabric for comfort that accented their finer quality when the collar was worn open. On 7 February 1966 DA directed that tan long-sleeve shirts be truncated. Effective 1 July 1966 only Tan shade 61 or Tan shade M-1 short-sleeve shirts could be worn with the army tan uniform without coat. During 1970 the durable-press Tan shade 445 shirt, made of polyester/rayon blended fabrics in open-collar fashion, was introduced.[7]

Khaki tropical worsted uniforms worn with helmet liners by **Brig. Gen. William Mitchell** (*left*) **and Sfc. Edward Fox** (*right*) **of the 5th Armd Div at Camp Chaffee, Arkansas, during an awards ceremony in June 1952. Trousers are bloused above cap-toe "paratrooper-style" russet combat boots.**

The Tan shade 61 long-sleeve shirt is worn with the black necktie by Lt. Col. Larkin Martin, Engineer Department director of the U.S. Army School Europe during 1965. Note name-plate on right pocket flap, distinctive insignia on shoulder loops, and collar insignia.

Maj. Gen. James Gavin (*right*) and other officers wear khaki tropical worsted uniforms with garrison caps at Camp Zama, Japan, in October 1954. Lt. Gen. Thomas Hickey (*center*) has airborne insignia on right curtain of cap and Olive Drab shade 51 necktie tucked into shirt.

Uniform Accessories

Officers wore a service cap with soft roll grommet and a removable cover in matching tan fabric. A band of basket-weave braid in Tan shade 61 encircled the cap, which had a leather visor (slanted 45 degrees) in Russet shade 90 and a matching ⅜-inch-wide chin strap and head strap. The issue service cap for enlisted men, introduced in a new

form during 1946, consisted of one cap frame along with covers for each seasonal uniform (see chapter 5). NCOs purchased optional covers to match the fabric of their tan uniforms.

The tan garrison cap was worn in travel status and when prescribed by unit commanders, especially when the shirt was worn instead of the jacket as the outer garment. The cap was designed in standard fashion with a curtain trimmed with cord-

Officers wearing the khaki tropical worsted uniform meet at the Frankfurt, Germany, train station in June 1956. IX Corps shoulder sleeve insignia worn on right sleeve (*left*) signified former wartime unit, and 3d Armd Div insignia worn on left sleeve (*right*) showed current assignment.

Army green service cap worn with the army tan uniform by Maj. Gen. William Hennig at Fort Meade, Maryland, in September 1958. Note the combat leaders' (green tab) identification on shoulder loops and service ribbons on contrasting cloth background.

MSgt. Jessie Perry of the Berlin Command Honor Guard (*right*) wears tropical worsted uniform without coat, along with chrome-plated helmet with parachutist white chin strap, shoulder cord, white boot laces, and MP russet leather accessories during July 1956.

Officers wear the army tan (tropical worsted) uniform without coat and the army cotton uniform (*left*) at Fort Meade, Maryland, in August 1965. The Tan shade 61 shirts have sharply pressed creases compared to the easily wrinkled cotton uniform.

edge braid. This braid was in the branch color of the assigned unit for enlisted men, and was gold for generals, gold intermixed with black for commissioned officers, and silver intermixed with black for warrant officers.

Headgear color changed from tan in accordance with the Army transition to army green uniform accessories. The army green service cap and garrison cap (see chapter 6) became mandatory for officers on 1 May 1957, and officers were required to wear them after that time. Enlisted men wore the caps as they became available for issue, which was accomplished by 1 February 1958.[8]

The service hat was an olive drab felt "Stetson hat" adopted in 1964 for drill sergeants, who were NCO graduates of a drill sergeant school at a U.S. Army training center, and assigned to a basic combat training platoon as either the principal trainers (senior drill sergeants) or trainers (drill sergeants). The service hat was worn in conjunction with the individual equipment belt, and the metal drill sergeant's identification badge was placed on the upper right pocket. Drill sergeants wore the 10-ounce Tan shade M-1 shirts.

The black leather strap, issued with the hat, was threaded through the appropriate eyelets in the

United Nations Honor Guard Lt. James DeRoos (*left*) wears the army tan uniform with white distinctive trimmings at Seoul, Korea, in July 1967. Note parachutist helmet liner with enamel finish and U.S. flag insignia, as well as M1902 officers' saber and decorative pistol lanyard.

Drill sergeants were authorized issue of the army tan uniform and distinctive items, including the olive drab felt service hat, as worn by Sfc. Robert Owens in October 1964. Note Expert Infantryman Badge.

SSgt. Wilson Provost wears the issue 10-ounce army tan shirt and trousers for drill sergeants during 1968. Note service hat, teal blue scarf, individual equipment belt, and Drill Sergeants' identification badge on right pocket.

The durable-press Tan shade 445 shirt, made of polyester/rayon blended fabrics, is worn by 339th Engineer Bn commander William Horn at Fort Lewis, Washington, during 1970. The short-sleeve shirt did not have a neck button and was worn without necktie.

brim of the hat, so that the strap passed around the front of the hat and the buckle was fastened and centered on the back of the wearer's head. The running end of the strap was to the wearer's left. The hat brim was worn level.[9]

The Rifle Green shade 297 wool beret ("green beret") was officially authorized for all personnel assigned to Special Forces units on 10 December 1961. The beret was made of melton cloth from quality knitted wool.

The field coat could be worn over the shirt, as directed by appropriate commanders, commencing 1 October 1969. The optional Army Green shade 274 wind-breaker, adopted in June 1970, was also authorized for the uniform. The wind-breaker was made of 5-ounce cotton/nylon cloth in lightweight jacket style. A rayon bib-type scarf in branch-of-service color could be worn beneath the outer garment collar. Whenever the long-sleeved tan shirt was worn as the outer garment and a neck-

The army tan uniform without coat is worn by Col. Lew Whiting, commander of the U.S. Modern Pentathlon Training Center at Fort Sam Houston, Texas, in May 1968. He is flanked by Pentathlon members in authorized military athletic attire.

tie was used, the necktie was tucked between the second and third buttons.[10]

The Khaki shade 5 cotton-mohair necktie, adopted during World War II, was worn until the Army switched to the cotton-mohair necktie in Olive Drab shade 51 (dark green) in 1948. The latter necktie was worn until 1 May 1957, when the black four-in-hand necktie was introduced in tropical worsted or other similar woven fabrics, or knitted fabric commencing in 1963. An optional pre-tied, snap-on necktie was permitted by DA regulations effective 5 April 1962.

Commercial suspenders could be worn underneath the tan coat, and the waist belt was required only when the shirt replaced the coat as the outer garment. The Olive Drab shade 3 waist belt with GCM buckle was authorized after 1948. The olive green or khaki web belts were optional. Effective 29 August 1957 officers were required to wear a black web or optional woven-elastic belt, and this requirement was extended to all ranks by 15 April 1959.[11]

Footwear included russet low-quarter service shoes or plain-toe blucher oxford-pattern shoes until 1 September 1956, when black low-quarter shoes were mandated. Commercial black leather shoes in plain toe, blucher oxford, chukka boot, or similar design were also permitted. Combat boots were worn when prescribed.

1. Palm Beach was a registered trademark of Goodall-Sanford Inc. Its famous summer suits combined "wrinkle-shedding" Palm Beach fabrics with distinctive tailoring that was associated with the best quality attire. For example, in 1957 the Palm Beach "Springweave" blend of 40 percent baby Angora mohair and fine virgin wool provided a full-bodied natural resiliency that made their suits light enough for warm weather yet equally comfortable during cool months.
2. AR 670-5, Para. 49, 28 September 1959.
3. AR 670-5, Change 5, 10 March 1965, and AR 670-5, Para. 6-1, 12 February 1968.
4. DA Circular 670-8, 29 September 1969.
5. U.S. Army Natick Laboratories, *Historical Report: FY 1970,* p. 56.
6. MIL-S-3011.
7. DA Circular 670-40, 3 September 1959, and DA Circular 670-1, 7 February 1966.
8. AR 670-5, Change 1, 17 December 1956, and Change 13, 1 February 1958.
9. CONARC Regulation 670-5, Para. 5, 1 July 1966.
10. AR 670-5, Change 1, 1 October 1969, and AR 670-5, Appendix A, 8 January 1971.
11. AR 670-5, Change 10, 29 August 1957.

8

Army Khaki Uniform

Uniform Utilization

The army khaki cotton uniform, composed of Khaki shade 1 cotton twill shirt and trousers, was the traditional mainstay of summer garrison duty attire. The Army color of Khaki shade 1 was reserved for the 100 percent cotton twill of the uniform. The hue was a light beige-brown color that was, as one veteran described it, "a drab color that looked warm on a hot summer day."[1]

Cotton twill khaki clothing required strict personal maintenance by each soldier. This was characterized by almost daily cleaning and starching of the uniform to present a suitable military appearance. As a result, the serviceman paid meticulous attention to the care and cleaning of his uniform. Garrison conditions enabled unit commanders to demand and expect this level of uniform perfection, which increased the soldier's pride in his personal appearance and his work.

The visible status of khaki-clad troops was higher than those wearing the other uniforms for two reasons. Army cotton khaki was the seasonal duty uniform for all ranks, and most Army units were stationed in posts where summertime conditions prevailed. In addition, this apparel was worn for both military reviews and civil unrest, when troop appearance was of paramount importance, and most activity of this nature occurred during warmer months.

The original army khaki uniform was worn with khaki headgear and khaki or olive drab necktie and olive drab waist belt, along with russet shoes or boots. The uniform's appearance was thoroughly changed when these items were replaced by army green uniform accessories. Footwear was changed to black in September 1956, and during the following year black waist belts, black neckties, and army green headgear were introduced.

Officers were directed to change according to strict DA scheduling, while enlisted supply distribution periods allowed for procurement delays. Soldiers appeared with either the old or the new sets of accessories during the transition from the khaki, olive drab, and russet accessories to army green and black, but different colors were never intermixed on the same uniform. The conversion was completed effective 1 October 1960.[2]

The original khaki summer uniform included a long-sleeve shirt and trousers. On 1 July 1956 DA created the "abbreviated cotton uniform" as a second or alternate category. The new category included a khaki cotton short-sleeve shirt, khaki cot-

The army khaki cotton Class A summer uniform is worn by Lt. William Hackett during August 1947. The Khaki shade 5 cotton-mohair necktie, worn until 1948, was tucked between the second and third buttons of the shirt. Note the Olive Drab shade 3 web belt with GCM buckle.

Pvt. Frank Foulenfont of the 348th AAA Gun Bn at Fort Bliss, Texas, during 1948 wears the Class A summer khaki uniform and garrison cap, with branch-of-service cord edge braid, as well as the khaki cotton-mohair necktie. The enlisted collar insignia was added to the uniform in 1946.

Transportation Maj. George Heidt Jr. wears the cotton Khaki shade 1 shirt at Anniston Ordnance Depot, Alabama, in July 1954, with the Olive Drab shade 51 cotton-mohair necktie for the summer Class A uniform.

Soldiers of the 362d Quartermaster Bn are dressed in Class A summer khaki uniforms as they prepare to depart for the 1963 summer encampment at Fort Lee, Virginia. The Army Green shade 44 garrison caps and the black neckties, web belts, and shoes were phased in during 1956 to 1958.

ton shorts, and Sand shade 115 knee-length cotton socks. The Army had experimented with this form of dress for use in the tropics during World War II, but was forced to abandon the idea of a short-sleeve shirt and knee-length trousers during the war because of the lack of malaria protection. The Army reintroduced the shorts when civilian "bermuda shorts" were in vogue.[3]

The abbreviated khaki uniform was popular at first but restricted to warmer geographical regions. Off-duty wear was restricted to areas where men's shorts were considered appropriate during hot weather. The uniform variant remained an available summer category, but it quickly fell out of favor after civilian fashion abandoned the bermuda shorts look. On 5 April 1962 DA regulations declared that the uniform could no longer be worn in formation, and the Army ceased issue of the shorts.[4]

The final category of the army khaki uniform was created by combining the khaki short-sleeve shirt with conventional trousers. Commanders had the discretion of allowing wear of the short-sleeve khaki shirt with the trousers by 27 June 1957. With the introduction of the lightweight army green uniform, the wear of the long-sleeve shirt with necktie as the Class A summer uniform ceased. On 23 September 1966 DA regulations announced that the short-sleeve shirt was the only shirt permitted with the trousers. This action terminated the need for long-sleeve khaki shirts, and as a result, the sleeves were truncated by DA directive.[5]

Uniform Components

The khaki uniform shirt was made of 8.2-ounce cotton twill in Khaki shade 1. The styling reflected the Doolittle Board–inspired 1946-pattern khaki shirt that "democratized" postwar khaki uniforms. World War II officer shirt features were thus incorporated for all ranks. The shirt had a stand-up collar, shoulder loops, two breast pockets with buttoned flaps (a pencil pocket was added inside the left pocket), and long sleeves with one or two-button cuffs.

Fourth Army master sergeant at Fort Sill, Oklahoma, wears Class B summer khaki uniform and garrison cap with branch-of-service cord-edge braid. Note non-issue cotton khaki chevrons.

The army green service cap with hard roll grommet is worn with Khaki shade 1 shirt with two-button cuff by Sgt. Maj. James Wiley at Fort Sill, Oklahoma, in August 1964. Compare khaki cotton shirt with sharply creased army tan tropical worsted shirt worn by Lt. Col. Robinson (*left*).

The army green service cap with soft roll grommet is worn with the Khaki shade 1 shirt by Sfc. Edward Ziebold (*right*) at Fort Sill, Oklahoma, in August 1964.

Transportation Sp4 Louis Moore of Fort Campbell, Kentucky, wears Khaki shade 1 shirt during August 1966. The enlisted branch-of-service insignia was aligned with the front leading edge of the collar of shirt.

Combat engineers in army khaki uniform "parade order" pass the HQ guidon of the 91st Engineer Bn at Fort Belvoir in 1961. Note M1 helmet liner, individual equipment belt, and trousers bloused above cap-toe black combat boots.

Army khaki Class B summer uniform is worn with camouflage scarf by First Sergeant Thompson, 326th Engineer Bn (101st Abn Div), at Fort Campbell, Kentucky, in May 1965. Note combat leaders' (green tab) identification on shoulder loops and parachutist badge on background trimming (oval).

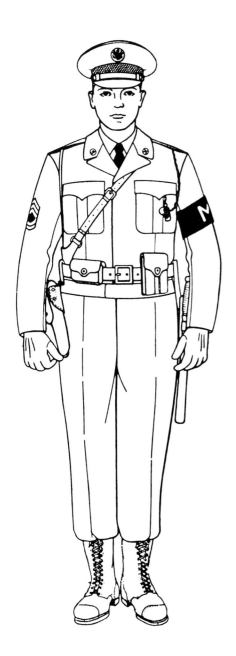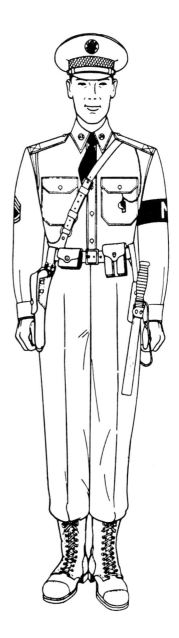

Olive drab wool serge uniform (*left*) and cotton khaki uniform shown with MP white service cap, MP brassard, whistle and chain, leather belt and shoulder strap supporting a pistol holster, double-magazine ammunition pocket, field first aid dressing case, and M1944 wooden policemen's club in carrier.

The abbreviated summer uniform, adopted in 1956, consisted of Khaki shade 1 cotton short-sleeve shirt and shorts, and Sand shade 115 knee-length cotton socks. The uniform is worn with army green service cap and black web belt and shoes. Note the early stitched creases in the cotton shorts.

The abbreviated summer khaki uniform, compared to the conventional Class B khaki uniform, is worn with army green service headgear by officers of the 2d Bn, 13th Artillery, at Fort Sill, Oklahoma, during 1958.

SSgt. Stanley Moskwa of the 1st Logistical Command in Vietnam wears army khaki as a duty uniform while checking data cards at the 14th Inventory Control Center in Saigon during January 1966. Note position of enlisted insignia of rank.

Soldiers at Fort Lewis, Washington, wear the 1955-pattern Khaki shade 1 short-sleeve shirt with box-pleat pockets and pointed flaps during August 1967. Note position of 339th Engineer Bn distinctive insignia on front left curtain of Army Green shade 44 garrison cap.

A short-sleeve khaki uniform shirt was produced according to specifications of 19 December 1955. The shirt was introduced as a component of the abbreviated khaki cotton uniform on 1 July 1956 and became a mandatory item of khaki attire commencing 1 July 1958.[6]

The shirt was made of 8.2-ounce cotton twill in Khaki shade 1. It was designed with an open-style collar without a neck button. The shirt had shoulder loops, two box-pleat pockets with buttoned pointed flaps, and a square bottom with side vents at the hem. Later the shirt was modified to simplify production and to conform to Army-style conventional shirt patterns. The box-pleat and pointed flaps were eliminated from the pocket design.

Effective 1 July 1966 the long-sleeve khaki uniform shirt was prohibited for wear with the uniform. On 7 February 1966, in anticipation of this change, DA directed soldiers to truncate long-sleeve shirts. This modification was accomplished by cutting the sleeves off evenly, turning under the raw edge, and stitching a new hem. The hem was set high enough to prevent the sleeve edge from wrinkling in the bend of the elbow.[7]

The conventional khaki uniform trousers were also made of 8.2-ounce cotton twill in Khaki shade 1. The design was standard, without pleats or cuffs, and contained two side pockets, two slit-type hip pockets, a watch pocket that was later eliminated, and a button or slide-fastened fly closure. The first pattern of trousers had a self-waistband with narrow belt loops. Later versions had a set-on waistband with wide belt loops.

The khaki cotton shorts, made of the same material as conventional trousers, were produced under specifications adopted on 28 October 1955. They were first issued on 1 July 1956 as a component of the abbreviated khaki uniform, and were only worn in this fashion. The prescribed length of the khaki shorts was 1 to 2 inches above the knee cap. The shorts were initially produced with sewn-in creases, but this feature hampered cleaning and was discarded in May 1957.[8]

The army khaki uniform is worn in highly personalized style by Maj. Gen. James Alger, CG of U.S. Army Forces Southern Command, at Fort Grant in Panama in August 1965. He has green service cap, camouflage scarf, and trousers bloused into Dehner tanker boots.

Army khaki uniform with the individual equipment belt with M1956 field dressing case is worn by Lt. Col. Edwin Beers (*left*) and Sgt. Maj. Henry Lee (*center*) of the 11th Inf Bde at Schofield Barracks, Hawaii, in September 1966. Note stand-up collar shirt with truncated sleeves.

The simplified pattern khaki short-sleeve shirt with clip-cornered pockets is worn with trousers bloused above combat boots by these troops of the 22d Aviation Bn at Fort Lewis during August 1969. Note starching of uniform and the bulk of the shirt at the waistline.

The simplified pattern khaki short-sleeve shirt is worn with khaki trousers and low-quarter shoes by soldiers of the 602d General Service Company during July 1972. Note how the trousers were often worn below the waistline.

Colonel Lawson of the Infantry School at Fort Benning, Georgia, wears 1955-pattern Khaki shade 1 short-sleeve shirt with Army Green shade 44 garrison cap at Fort Benning, Georgia, during 1964. Note airborne insignia on right curtain of garrison cap and position of officer insignia of grade and branch.

Ordnance Sp4 Michael Bell of Fort Lee, Virginia, wears the simplified pattern Khaki shade 1 shirt during July 1971. Note the position of enlisted collar insignia worn perpendicular to the leading edge of the shirt collar.

Uniform Accessories

The original headgear with the army khaki uniform was a service cap in matching fabric. Officers wore a cap with a soft-roll grommet and a removable cover. A band of basket-weave braid in Khaki shade 1 encircled the cap, which had a leather visor (slanted 45 degrees) in Russet shade 90 and a matching ⅝-inch-wide chin strap and head strap. The issue service cap for enlisted men, introduced in a new form during 1946, consisted of one cap frame along with covers for each seasonal uniform

(see chapter 5). The removable cotton cover could be laundered and stretched.

The M1950 garrison cap was of standard curtain design without a gusset along the center seam. It was worn in travel status and when prescribed by unit commanders. During times of mobilization, the service cap was not issued because of cost and convenience, and the garrison cap served instead as the principal headgear.

The garrison cap was made of matching Khaki shade 1 cotton twill fabric and had cord-edge braid along its upturned curtain. This braid was in the branch color of the assigned unit for enlisted men, and was gold for generals, gold intermixed with black for commissioned officers, and silver intermixed with black for warrant officers.

Headgear color changed from khaki in accordance with the Army transition to army green uniform accessories. The army green service cap and garrison cap (see chapter 6) became mandatory for officers on 1 May 1957, and officers were required to wear them after that time. Enlisted men wore the caps as they became available for issue, which was accomplished by 1 February 1958.[9]

The service hat and green beret were worn as described in chapter 7. A rayon bib-type scarf in branch-of-service color could be worn, beneath the collar of the shirt. White gloves could also be worn on those ceremonial occasions as prescribed by commanding officers.

The field coat, or field jacket, could be worn over the shirt, as directed by appropriate commanders, commencing 1 October 1969. The Army Green shade 274 wind-breaker was authorized to be worn with the army khaki uniform on an optional basis after June 1970. The wind-breaker was made out of 5-ounce cotton/nylon cloth in lightweight jacket style.[10]

Army khaki Class B summer uniform worn with helmet liners by firing party detail of the 688th Engineer Company in Houma, Louisiana, during military funeral services in 1965. Trousers are bloused above combat boots.

Army khaki uniform is worn by color guard at Fort Benning, Georgia, with chrome-plated helmets and white accessories. The color sergeants carry the national and organizational colors with adjustable web color slings.

Color Guard of the 91st Engineer Bn at Fort Belvoir, Virginia, in 1969 in khaki uniform with chrome-plated helmets, white gloves, and white M1936 web pistol belts. The color sergeants wear adjustable web color slings.

Military Police color guard at Fort Meade, Maryland, during June 1966. This view shows the MP white service cap and white cotton gloves of the color bearers. Note back detail of khaki uniform shirt and trousers of Staff Sergeant Baily (*right*).

The necktie was first worn with the long-sleeve shirt for Class A summer uniforms. It was required to be tucked between the second and third buttons of the shirt. The World War II Khaki shade 5 cotton/mohair necktie was worn initially. Start-ing in 1948 the Army switched to the dark green Olive Drab shade 51 cotton/mohair necktie on an optional basis, and its wear became mandatory by 1951. This necktie was worn until the black four-in-hand necktie was prescribed in tropical worsted

The 306th MP Company (Escort Guard) have pistols inspected before going on duty in 1962. Each carries the M1944 wooden policemen's club with leather thong in carriers on the left hip. Note pistol magazine in belt and white pistol lanyard (*left*) looped over right shoulder.

Members of the 895th MP Company on Okinawa during October 1969 wear the M1955-pattern khaki shirt with the dark blue MP brassard, used both as identification and a symbol of authority. Note the plastic-finish white military police service caps and MP leather belts.

Military policeman at Fort Riley, Kansas, in 1965 wears army khaki uniform with MP accessories. These consist of black leather belt and shoulder strap supporting a pistol holster, double-magazine ammunition pocket, and field first aid dressing case. Note how collar tended to curl if not worn with commercial collar stays.

or other similar woven, or knitted commencing in 1963, fabrics. The transition to the black tie was accomplished starting 1 May 1957. DA permitted wearing an optional pre-tied snap-on necktie, effective 5 April 1962.

After 1948 the waist belt was the Olive Drab shade 3 web belt with GCM buckle. Khaki or olive green web belts were optional. On 29 August 1957 officers were directed to wear a black web or optional woven-elastic belt. On 13 June 1958 the belt became available for enlisted wear, except in formation. On 1 October 1958 the belt became part of initial clothing issues, and on 15 April 1959 the black belt officially replaced the olive drab belt. The individual equipment belt, or web pistol belt, was worn to designate special status, or in formations and reviews as explained in chapter 7.[11]

Army khaki uniform components are worn with black baseball caps and trousers bloused into combat boots by parachute instructors at the Fort Campbell Airborne School during May 1956. Note quarter-sleeve undershirt worn with unit insignia.

Khaki breeches and legging-top leather boots are worn with gloves and riding cap by riding instructor Pvt. Bill Robertson of the U.S. Modern Pentathlon Training Center at Fort Sam Houston, Texas, during June 1966.

A modified army khaki uniform is worn with breeches and service hats by drivers and cannoneers of a ceremonial field artillery caisson team during a review at Fort Sam Houston, Texas, in October 1966.

The Sand shade 115 knee-length socks were introduced as a component of the abbreviated khaki cotton uniform on 1 July 1956. These socks were only worn with the khaki cotton shorts and became a mandatory khaki item on 1 July 1958. The seamless socks were made of combed two-ply cotton knitting and nylon reinforcing yarn. They were worn about 1 inch below the bottom of the knee cap, and had a turnover of about 2½ or 3 inches at the top.[12]

Footwear consisted of russet low-quarter blucher oxford-pattern shoes or combat service boots until 1 September 1956, when black shoes or combat boots became required. Tan socks with low-quarter shoes were also changed to black at the same time.

1. The army khaki uniform was designated the khaki uniform until 1956, the cotton uniform until 1959, and thereafter the army khaki uniform.
2. AR 670-5, Change 1, 17 December 1956, and AR 670-5, Para. 66, 28 September 1959.
3. DA Circular 670-4, 22 March 1956. American tourists brought the knee-length bermuda shorts style back from Bermuda, where the law required shorts to come within 2 inches of the knee, for golf and tennis. The fashion was extended to informal dances or country clubs by the summer of 1953. Civilian dictates had always mandated that bermuda shorts be worn with knee-length socks. The ensuing Army adoption of this style actually transpired after its civilian fashionability faded.
4. AR 670-5, Change 2, 5 April 1962.
5. AR 670-5, Change 9, 27 June 1957, and AR 670-5, Para. 5–6, 23 September 1966.
6. DA Circular 670-4, 22 March 1956.
7. DA Circular 670-1, 7 February 1966.
8. DA Circular 670-4, 22 March 1956, and DA Circular 670-13, 7 May 1957.
9. AR 670-5, Change 1, 17 December 1956; Change 13, 1 February 1958; and AR 670-5, Change 4, 31 January 1957.
10. AR 670-5, Change 1, 1 October 1969, and AR 670-5, Appendix A, 8 January 1971.
11. AR 670-5, Change 10, 29 August 1957, and DA Circular 670-27, 13 June 1958.
12. DA Circular 670-4, 22 March 1956.

9

Field and Work Uniforms

HBT Clothing

Before World War II the Army sharply distinguished between field service attire and necessary work apparel. At the time of national mobilization, the soldiers' traditional work clothing, or "fatigues," consisted of blue denim one-piece and two-piece suits. This clothing was replaced by olive drab herringbone twill (HBT) outfits during the Army's resulting mechanization and wartime expansion. Throughout the global campaigning of World War II modified HBT attire functioned as a "battle dress" uniform for both work and combat purposes. The 1949 Uniform Board formally sanctioned this evolution by creating a separate uniform category, field and work clothing, that did not have to meet the requirements for garrison duty wear.

In 1949 this field work uniform consisted of a variety of HBT jacket and trouser combinations and one-piece HBT suits for mechanics. All these outfits continued to be worn well into the Cold War era. Several patterns were adopted through the years, but these coexisted within Army supply channels and issue was commonly intermixed. Thus, the various components were worn without

any styling conformity by officers and enlisted personnel alike.

The drafted-citizen Army of the postwar period used field and work clothing as its ordinary uniform for training and duty wear, which caused increased command emphasis on sharpening its military appearance. The upper garment was required to be tucked into the trousers, despite its jacket design, and trousers to be bloused over the boots. Furthermore, the uniform was routinely starched, form fitted, and even "match-faded" in numbered sets to achieve consistent coloration despite frequent laundering.

The HBT jacket, made of cotton herringbone twill in Olive Drab shade 7, was designed with a single-breasted button closure and a convertible collar. The wartime jacket contained upper cargo pockets or center-pleat pockets, while the simplified 1946 pattern had patch pockets. The HBT trousers had cargo or center-pleat side pockets that were replaced in late 1945 by front patch pockets. The original M1941 "burst of glory" metal tack buttons, in japanned black, were gradually replaced in postwar production by flat phenol formaldehyde (plastic) sew-on buttons in Olive Drab shade 6.

The "U.S. ARMY" distinguishing insignia

The Olive Drab shade 7 field cotton HBT uniform with field caps at Fort Benning, Georgia, in March 1952. The dark cotton (*center*) faded and required washing in matched sets (*right*) to avoid uniform disparity (*left*). Note 508th Abn RCT pocket patch (*center*) and 1st Armd Div insignia placement.

Maj. John Harkins of the 3d Inf Div in Korea during October 1954 wears stiffened field cap and HBT uniform with cargo-pocket trousers. His custom-tailored HBT jacket has center-pleat pockets, cuffs, and shoulder loops.

General officers wear customized HBT field uniforms modified with added shoulder loops in Korea during July 1954. They have blocked caps, scarves of camouflaged nylon parachute canopy fabric or blue silk, and swagger sticks. Note wide commercial "Ridgway buckle" (*right*).

Olive Green shade 108 wool shirt worn with HBT field trousers (*left*) contrasts with the field outfit of PFC James Ingram of the 33d Scout Dog Platoon, Seventh Army, in Grafenwoehr, Germany, during June 1955. Both wear field caps instead of utility caps. Dog handler leather leash strap is on belt. Note U.S. Army distinguishing insignia above left pocket, introduced in 1953.

was authorized on 27 October 1953 and worn above the left pocket on the jacket. The woven label had golden yellow block lettering on a black background. A name tape was added by local unit directives above the right pocket and contained the soldier's last name. Early name tapes were often in branch colors but most were made of white engineer tape with black lettering. Effective 14 July 1966 DA directed that both tapes have black lettering on Olive Green shade 107 cloth.[1]

Utility Uniforms

Textile research conducted during the Korean War led to the development of more durable cotton material with the same weight as herringbone twill. During 1952 this 8.5-ounce carded cotton sateen fabric was manufactured in Olive Green shade 107 and used to produce the new utility jacket and trouser combinations.

The Army used the official designation "utility" for this uniform, which was consistent with the terminology of other services. Army soldiers, however, continued to use the traditional term "fatigues" because of the "fatiguing" duty performed while wearing the uniform. The utility or fatigue clothing was intended to be loose fitting, although the shirt was normally worn tucked into the trousers, and the trousers were bloused when wearing combat boots.[2]

The Olive Green shade 107 cotton utility jacket was produced under specifications dated 30

The HBT clothing was styled loosely for field movement, and the ample cargo pockets could hold a variety of items in addition to the K-ration boxes they were designed for, as shown by Maj. Gen. Hobart Hewett of UNC Military Assistance Command in August 1954.

(*Right*) Sergeant First Class Berhow displays M60 machine gun. He wears helmet liner and first-pattern cotton sateen jacket with straight pocket flaps and pocket patch of 1st Battle Group, 28th Inf, at Fort Riley, Kansas, during 1960. The officers (*right*) wear commercial cotton sateen shirts with shoulder loops.

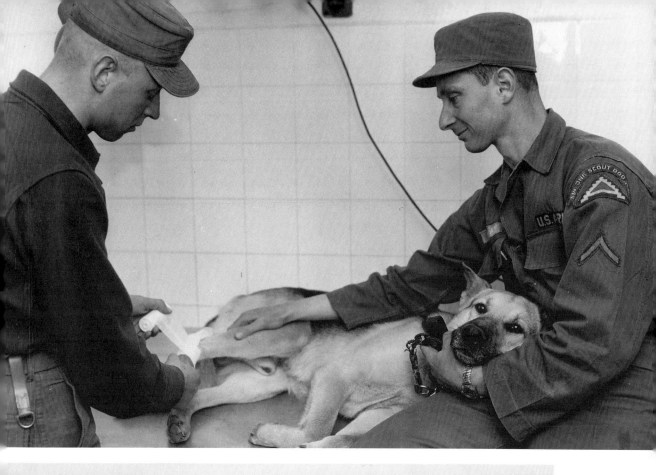

Lt. Col. Merlyn Smith of the 2d Bn, 13th Artillery, wears helmet liner and first-pattern cotton sateen jacket and trousers during an awards ceremony at Fort Sill, Oklahoma, in May 1962.

Sp4 Richard Cravens (*right*) wears the cotton sateen trousers, showing the standard hip patch pocket design with straight flaps. The trouser side patch pocket is visible on Lt. Col. Merlyn Smith (*left*) during the same Fort Sill ceremony.

Artillery maintenance warrant officers wear first-pattern cotton sateen uniforms. The belt metal tip is placed "brass on brass" with polished GCM buckle. Note 1957-pattern warrant officer insignia of rank on blocked cap of C.W.O. Richard Hoffman (*left*), of the 2d Bn, 17th Artillery, at Fort Sill, Oklahoma, in June 1963.

SSgt. Willie Barker, a 25th Inf Div artillery section chief in Hawaii during 1963, wears a commercial OG-106 utility "baseball" cap with first-pattern cotton sateen uniform. His trousers are bloused with combat boots. Note 8-inch towed howitzer.

Starched first-pattern cotton sateen jacket and trousers worn with helmets by artillerymen of the 6th Bn, 27th Arty, at Fort Bliss, Texas, during 1964. Helmet cover (*left*) has camouflage helmet band. Individual equipment belts are worn with first aid dressing/magnetic compass cases.

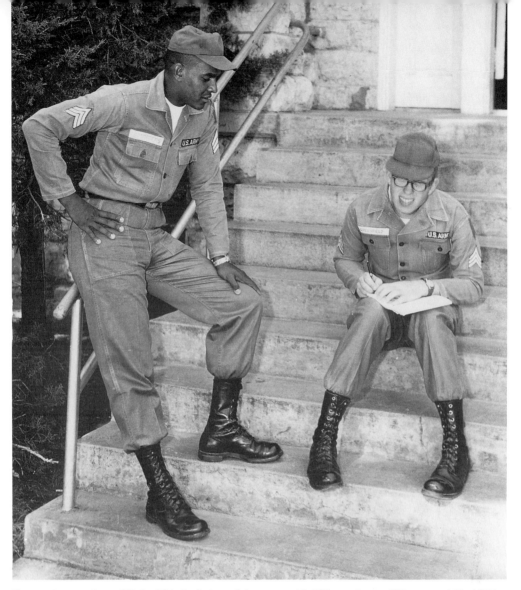

Sergeants wear form-fitted utility jackets and trousers with PX-purchase utility caps at Fort Riley, Kansas, during 1965. Commercial elastic garters are used for blousing the trousers over black leather combat boots.

August 1952. It had straight sleeves and upper patch pockets with rectangular buttoned flaps. The matching cotton utility trousers were produced under specifications dated 21 November 1952. The trousers had large side patch pockets, two hip patch pockets with buttoned rectangular flaps, and size adjustment tabs. Although the trouser design remained consistent, the utility jacket underwent several minor specification changes.

The Olive Green shade 107 cotton sateen

shirt, produced under specifications dated 12 April 1963, replaced the utility jacket. The garment's appearance was improved by altering the button spacing and realigning the pockets to produce a higher neck opening. In addition, the shirt had clipped-cornered pockets in conformity with other Army shirts.[3]

Further continuity in distinctive army styling was adversely affected by the consolidation of military supply activities at the Department of De-

The field utility uniform is worn with **M1956 individual equipment belt and suspenders, canteen cover, and small arms ammunition case during tests of the Colt AR-15 in Hawaii during November 1965. Commercial elastic blousing garters are used to secure the trousers above the combat boot.**

The 1963-pattern OG-107 cotton shirt, with clip-cornered pockets and raised front buttons, during pistol practice at Fort Belvoir, Virginia, in September 1965. Note commercial utility cap (*right*) contrasted with issue OG-106 hot-weather cap (*third from right*).

The first-pattern cotton sateen jacket with full-cut sleeves worn with issue OG-106 hot-weather utility cap and combat boots (*left*) contrasts with the tropical combat uniform with Vietnamese-made utility cap and tropical combat boots, in Vietnam during 1967.

fense. This action was taken with the avowed purpose of adopting a more economical approach, in order to provide universal military patterns for all the armed forces. This trend became apparent in 1964, when the Army adopted a new utility shirt.

The Olive Green shade 107 utility shirt, produced under specifications dated 6 November 1964, was made of cotton sateen. It was designed with patch pockets and pointed flaps, buttoned cuffs, and new-style concave dull plastic buttons. The pocket designs were similar to those used on Navy and Marine Corps garments. The Air Force employed the same pattern in a cotton twill Blue shade 1549.[4]

In 1973 the Army began testing utility uniforms made of polyester/cotton material in Olive Green shade 507 with wash-and-wear advantages. This program resulted in the durable-press utility shirt, produced under specifications dated 25 August 1975, and the durable-press utility trousers, produced under specifications dated 10 October 1975. The revised clothing was easier to clean and maintain, especially in field and work settings. Many officers and NCOs, however, believed that the lack of crisp "military starching" was detrimental to its garrison duty appearance.

As field and work clothing, utility uniforms were worn with all authorized individual and organizational equipment. The use of "fatigues" as routine duty uniforms also subjected them to increased command emphasis. In order to enhance the appearance of the utility outfits, military personnel often undertook alterations such as form-fitting, the addition of shoulder loops, cuffs on straight-sleeve jackets, extra pockets, and other modifications. These were routinely made, despite DA regulation prohibitions.

Following the Korean War, the emphasis on fatigue headgear was placed on its appearance rather than function. The Olive Green shade 107 cap was introduced with the cotton sateen utility uniform in 1952, but its appearance was considered unacceptable. In addition, since the cap was worn during basic training, it was branded as

The open sleeves of the first-pattern cotton sateen jacket (*right*) permitted a crisp military appearance in contrast to the buttoned cuffs of the utility shirt, during awards ceremony of the 283d Avn Co, 5th Army, at Fort Carson, Colorado, in March 1967. Note distinctive ascots being worn.

Unsubdued insignia sewn on commercial cotton sateen jacket is displayed by 25th Inf Div Capt. Allison Vickery in Cu Chi, Vietnam, during September 1966. He has Combat Infantryman Badge and parachutist badge over U.S. Army distinguishing insignia, and Vietnam Special Purpose Forces parachute badge over name tape.

The utility shirt introduced in 1964 had V-cut pocket flaps and new-style dull concave plastic buttons. It is worn with sewn-on subdued insignia and yellow branch-of-service scarf by 6th Armored Cavalry Regiment Capt. David Powers at Fort Meade, Maryland, in August 1969.

Maj. John Hall of the 91st Engineer Bn has unsubdued cloth insignia, including army aviator badge and parachutist badge, sewn on his modified cotton sateen jacket at Fort Belvoir, Virginia, in September 1967. Note white name tape and U.S. Army distinguishing insignia.

the sign of a fresh recruit. The issue M1951 cotton field cap was worn instead with the fatigue uniform, but measures to improve its appearance proved unsatisfactory. These included the addition of cardboard stiffeners under the inside folded earflaps or the substitute use of the commercial blocked cap, such as the unlaunderable Louisville Cap Corporation "Spring-up" cap. All these stiff caps were difficult to pack and impossible to launder.

The Army design conflict between function and appearance hampered development of a new cap. Throughout 1956 and 1957 the Army consid-

Crew members of a CH-54 "Flying Crane" helicopter wear third-pattern utility uniforms at Heidelberg, Germany. Senior NCO and officers' uniforms (*center*) benefitted from expensive laundering and contrast with the light starching of the enlisted uniform (*right*).

ered reintroduction of the "Austrian-style" ski caps of the M1943 experimental combat outfit, which were redesignated as T58-series caps. During 1958 DA established a headgear design study group to select a new basic cap, and appearance was given top priority. This action resulted in the testing of seven different cap designs, known as the T59 series.

The T59 series of caps included the T59-2 baseball, T59-3 forager, T59-4 ski, T59-5 stand-up

(a modified stiffened cotton field cap), T59-6 frame with detachable cover, T59-9 commercial fold-up style cap, and T59-10 adjustable golf cap. The last was found most acceptable by the Continental Army Command (CONARC), but higher Army staff disapproved the cap's back opening and its adjustable band. On 9 June 1961 DA decided to use a modified baseball cap in different sizes.[5]

The modified baseball cap was tested in the

Signal specialist (*left*) and logistics lieutenant wear the 1964-pattern utility shirt with standard utility cap at Sharpe Army Depot, California, in November 1971. Subdued pin-on metal insignia of grade are worn. Note the heavy starch of commercial laundering on right.

fall of 1961, and DA adopted it on 24 January 1962 as the Olive Green shade 106 hot-weather cap. It was made of polyester/rayon gabardine with a six-piece contour shaped crown, a nylon mesh stiffener at the front panels, and a long, flat rubber-interlined visor. Issue of the new utility cap began 1 November 1963, but dissatisfaction with its initial "beanie" design led many soldiers to purchase commercial variants. During 1969 the Army modified the utility cap by lowering the crown and improving the visor in an attempt to achieve acceptance by the troops.[6]

Utility headgear was also used for identifica-

tion and to designate jobs or positions. For example, white engineer tape was stapled around the crown of fatigue caps by instructors and referees during field exercises. Commercial baseball caps in solid colors were authorized for aircraft and ground crew members, among others, as a safety and identification measure. The service hat was also worn by drill sergeants and the green beret was worn by Special Forces, as explained in chapter 7.

The helmet liner, part of the M1 steel helmet assembly, served as alternate headgear for the utility uniform. The liner, when polished and affixed

The utility uniform is worn in prescribed "heat category" manner, outside the trousers with sleeves rolled up, by VII Corps commander Lt. Gen. George Blanchard (*left*), wearing 1964-pattern utility shirt, and 34th Signal Bn Sergeant First Class Paige in 1963-pattern OG-107 cotton shirt at Ludwigsburg, Germany, during 1973.

DI Sfc. Edward McGinnis wears 1964-pattern utility shirt with the service hat worn by drill sergeants during instruction at Fort Polk, Louisiana, in 1970. Drill sergeants received extra allowances of clothing to maintain a professional military image.

The 1969-pattern polyester/cotton utility uniform in Olive Green shade 507 provided a low-maintenance alternative that gradually replaced the cotton sateen utility uniform. It was worn first by officers and senior NCOs. Note the subdued frame buckle that replaced the GCM buckle for the field and work uniform.

with insignia, formed unit parade headgear and also identified special personnel. For instance, painted bands were often used by military police, officer candidates, and training cadre.

After 1948 the issue waist belt was the Olive Drab shade 3 version with GCM buckle. Khaki shade 1 and olive green elastic web belts, with plain solid brass buckles, were also worn. On 29

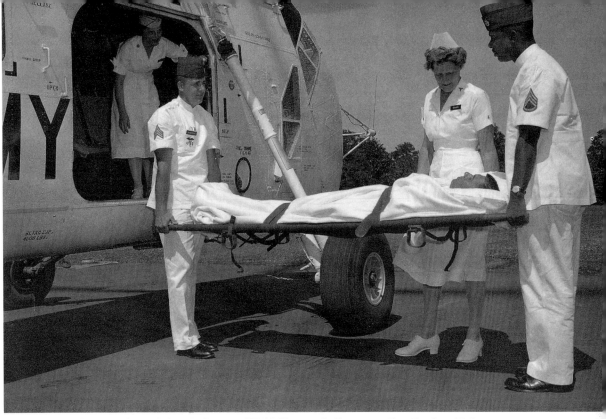

Medical specialists transfer an injured pilot to a CH-34 Choctaw helicopter at Fort Rucker, Alabama, in 1963. They wear white hospital duty clothing and green garrison caps. Note white hospital duty dress of the Army nurse.

White medical assistants' smock is worn at Fort Hayes, Colorado, during April 1965. The U.S. caduceus insignia was imprinted on right pocket of the jacket.

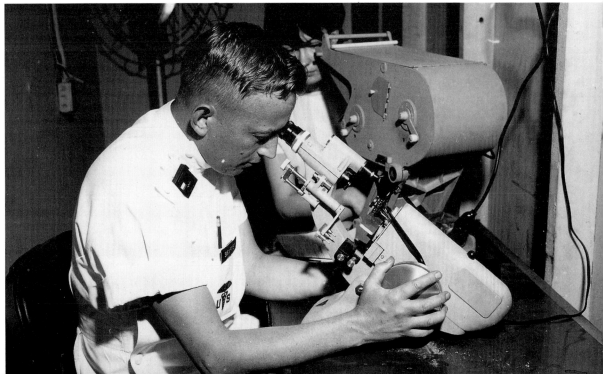

Work clothing for food handler personnel at Fort Jackson, South Carolina, in September 1969. Note white paper hats.

FRONT　　　　　　　　　　　　BACK

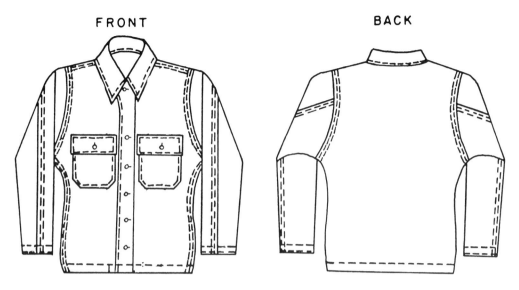

Olive Green shade 107 cotton sateen utility jacket, 1952.

August 1957 officers were required to wear a black web or optional woven-elastic belt, and in 1959 this requirement was extended to all ranks. The prewar open-faced or frame buckle was intended for combat, and its issue was stopped during the postwar era. The frame buckles remained as a mobilization supply item and were reintroduced with a black finish on a widespread basis during the Vietnam era.[7]

The natural brown combat service boot or "suede buckle boot," with reverse-uppers and buckled cuffs, was replaced at the end of the Korean War by the fully laced 1948-pattern russet combat boot. The boot was 10½ inches high, had a

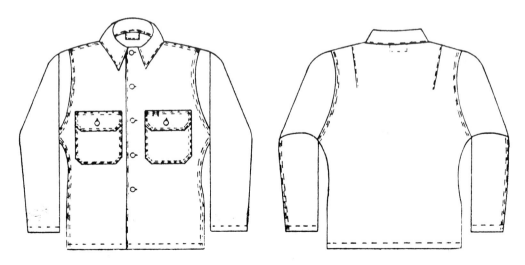

Olive Green shade 107 cotton sateen shirt, 1963.

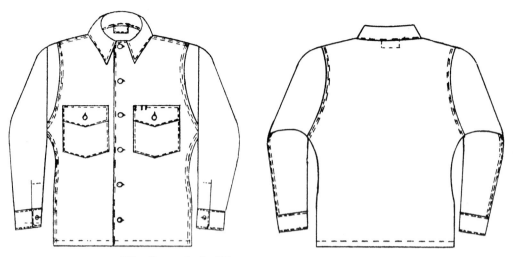

Olive Green shade 107 cotton sateen utility shirt, 1964.

Goodyear-welt diamond-tread sole, and featured a "paratrooper style" cap toe. On 1 September 1956 the Army began the transition to black footwear, and a DA circular of 12 January 1958 provided instructions for applying commercial dye to the russet-colored combat boots for this purpose.[8]

During 1962 the black leather combat boot of a new design was adopted as part of the standardization of supply throughout the armed forces, and was known disparagingly as the "McNamara boot" after Secretary of Defense Robert Strange McNamara. The design lowered the boot height to 8½ inches and removed the cap toe, which had been a source of spit-shined pride to all soldiers. During January 1967 the direct molded sole (DMS) black leather combat boot was adopted, which deleted the Goodyear welt sole and incorporated a new rubber compound process first used in the tropical combat boot, and changed the sole to a chevron-tread design.

Wool Field Uniforms

For winter field service, the Army authorized Olive Green shade 108 wool/nylon field shirts and trousers. These were developed during the Korean conflict to replace the Army's previous olive drab wool shirts and trousers, but not distributed widely until after the armistice.

When the clothing became available, commanders of units in colder regions often classified them as locally approved winter duty uniforms because of their superior military styling and warmth. Army regulations permitted commanders to designate appropriate field organizational clothing in this manner.

As a result, the olive green wool/nylon shirt and trousers essentially functioned as a winter equivalent of the army khaki duty uniform, despite DA admonishments to reserve the clothing for proper field use, The shirts were often modified by form-fitting and the addition of shoulder loops and sleeve and pencil pockets with flap closures.

The olive green wool/nylon shirt and trousers, however, were not intended as exterior garments, but to be worn underneath the cotton field coat and trouser shells as basic components of the cold-weather clothing system. The clothing lost insulating qualities if it became wet or matted with dirt. The 16-ounce shrink-resistant wool/nylon flannel shirting cloth tended to soil quickly, become snagged, and sustain damage. The loose-fitting garments were adjusted by darts and tabs for sizing, and their field flexibility was negated whenever tailored.

The Olive Green shade 108 wool/nylon shirt was first produced under specifications approved on 22 January 1951. It had upper patch pockets with buttoned flaps (with a silesia-cloth pencil

The Olive Green shade 108 wool/nylon field uniform was designed to be worn as part of the cold-weather clothing ensemble, but its good military appearance led to widespread local authorization as a winter duty uniform. It is worn with the OG-107 field cap during July 1959.

Brig. Gen. Donald Grothaus wears the olive green wool/nylon uniform, M1951 pile field cap, general officers' belt and gold-plated buckle, with holster attached, as he exits a CH-34 "Choctaw" helicopter in 1962. White engineer tape is used for name tape.

Sergeants of the 4th Inf Div wear Olive Green shade 108 field shirts with cotton poplin field clothing beside division commander Major General Hutchin in field coat (*center*) during Operation Polar Siege in Alaska, in December 1963. They have military skis and ski poles.

pocket in the left front pocket), buttoned cuffs, and a square bottom design to facilitate wearing outside the trousers under field conditions. The two darts, stitched in the back, could be ripped out to increase the width of the shirt at the waist.[9]

The Olive Green shade 108 trousers were made of 18-ounce wool and nylon serge. The trousers had outlets at the side seam, belt loops, suspender straps, waist adjustments, a buttoned fly closure, two side pockets, two flapped hip pockets, and one waistband lining pocket.[10]

The M1951 field trouser shells were made of

9-ounce wind-resistant, water-repellent cotton sateen cloth in Olive Green shade 107. They were normally worn as wind-breaker shells over the wool/nylon trousers during moderately cold weather, and as intermediate layers underneath the arctic trouser shells during colder conditions. The trouser shells were first produced under specifications approved on 15 November 1952, and contained waistband adjustments, suspender loops, a slide-fastened fly, and leg hem draw-cords. The shells had two front and two hip inside-hanging pockets with snap-closed flaps, and two side cargo

Pressed olive green field uniforms are worn for inspection under arms during a review of the 2d Armd Div at Fort Hood, Texas, in February 1966. The shoulder sleeve insignia, insignia of grade, and name tapes are added, while U.S. Army distinguishing insignia was placed by the manufacturer as part of shirt production.

Army COFS George Decker (*front row, center*) and VII Corps staff at the German-Czechoslovakian "Iron Curtain" border zone in May 1961. Field clothing includes blocked caps, olive green wool/nylon shirts tucked into cotton poplin field trousers, and bloused boots.

The olive green field uniform is worn by the Eighth Army Honor Guard in Korea during March 1970. It includes wool/nylon shirt and trousers, M1951 field pile caps, camouflage ascots, white gloves, and burnished parade pistol belts. Note hip pocket with concealed-button flap, characteristic of field trousers.

pockets with tie-cords. On 8 February 1957 they were revised as the M1951 Olive Green shade 107 cotton trouser shells, were later redesignated Olive Green shade 107 cotton poplin field trousers, and became Olive Green shade 107 cold weather field trousers effective 11 December 1970.[11]

The wool/nylon uniform was issued as organizational field clothing. Headgear, articles of individual equipment, waist belts, and footgear were identical to those allotted for wear with the utility uniform.

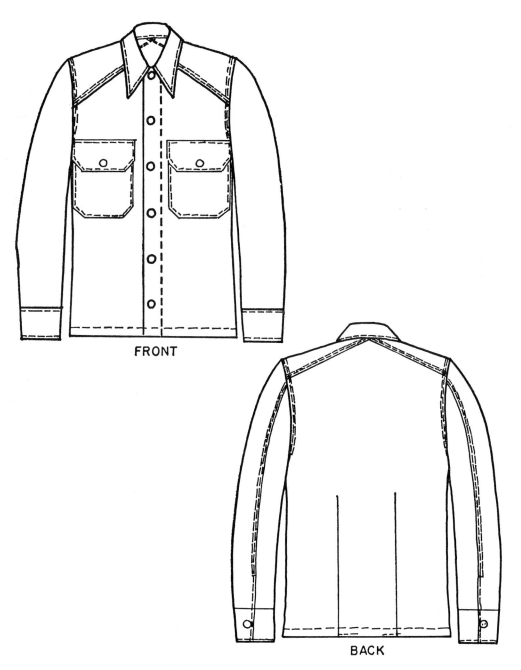

FRONT

BACK

Olive Green shade 108 wool/nylon shirt.

Tropical combat uniform worn under arms by 6th Inf Div soldiers at Schofield Barracks, Hawaii, during 1968. The third-pattern simplified uniform without shoulder loops is worn with individual equipment belts with quick-release buckles. Trousers are tucked into the tops of the combat boots.

Tropical and Desert Combat Uniforms

Just as the Army had developed special winter field uniforms for use in World War II and the Korean War, combat operations in Southeast Asia necessitated battlefield clothing for hot weather. The Army approved specifications for the tropical combat uniform, or "jungle fatigues," on 20 June 1963. The uniform became the primary field clothing for Army personnel stationed in tropical or semi-tropical regions of Asia and Central and South America. It became the general duty uniform in the Vietnam combat zone on 27 October 1967.[12]

The tropical combat coat and trousers were made of lightweight 5.5-ounce cotton poplin fabric in Olive Green shade 107 or later Army Engineer Research and Development Laboratory (ERDL) camouflage coloration. The coat was a loose fitting "bush jacket" style that was fitted with waist-adjusting side tabs and shoulder loops. The two upper bellows pockets were in slanted position and the lower bellows pockets were straight. The 1963-pattern coat contained exposed buttons on the pockets, side tabs, and shoulder loops. On 26 August 1964 specifications were adopted for a coat with concealed buttons. Following the conclusion of the uniform board in Vietnam during 1965, a simplified version of the tropical combat coat was recommended. Accordingly, on 29 December 1966 specifications were adopted that deleted the side tabs and shoulder loops.[13]

The tropical combat trousers were designed with two front inside-hanging pockets, two hip pockets, two bellows cargo pockets on the trouser sides, and either a slide-fastened or button fly. The bottom of the trouser legs were fitted with tunneled draw cords for tighter fitting around footwear while giving flexibility for water drainage and ventilation.

The tropical hat, also designated by DA as the hot-weather hat, was known as the "bush" or

Second-pattern tropical combat uniform coat is worn with general officers' belt and buckle by 1st Cav Div commander Maj. Gen. George Putnam in Vietnam. Note combat leaders' "green tab" identification worn on shoulder loops, and pens placed into upper bellows pocket. Insignia is embroidered directly onto the coat.

SSgt. Larry Lingo of the 199th Inf Bde wears combat tropical uniform with trouser cargo pockets filled, at Nha Be, Vietnam, in February 1967. Note two MkIIA1 fragmentation hand grenades, secured by the straps on his universal small arms ammunition case.

Sgt. Daniel Huzinec of the 101st Abn Div wears the combat tropical uniform with the hot-weather or tropical hat, near Phuoc Vinh, Vietnam, in February 1968. He is filling his plastic 1-quart canteen with powdered fruit drink.

"boonie" hat. This hat was produced according to specifications approved on 20 December 1967. It was made of the same material as the coat and weighed 4 ounces with its detachable insect net. The design included a stitched full brim, screened eyelets, a headband sewn to permit openings for foliage insertion, and an adjustable chin strap with leather keeper.

By 1971 the Army had designed a uniform in tropical combat uniform styling for desert operations. The uniform consisted of coat, trousers, hat, and neckerchief in solid sand color for a daytime desert environment. An insulated layer was planned to give protection during the temperature drops that accompanied nighttime desert use.

Desert camouflaging of the uniform for further protection in hot-dry barren terrain was inhibited by concerns over undue heat stress. The main problem was the conflicting requirement for high reflectance by day, to reduce solar heat load, and high infrared absorption to counter detectors at night. A separation of these requirements was planned by designing an over-garment that added insulation for lower temperatures, with specific camouflage protection against night-viewing devices. DA began development of a six-color desert camouflage print, but it did not receive a procurement description until 1973.[14]

Aggressor Force Uniforms

During the years of the Cold War, the Army found it increasingly necessary to field a realistic opposition force. Aggressor forces were Army personnel dressed as soldiers of a mythical hostile power,

Aggressor force troops wear uniforms dyed jungle green with pullover tunic (*center*) and helmet liners fitted with wooden combs on the ridge. This attire is worn by the "Red Army" on a 4th Inf Div exercise near Yakima, Washington, during April 1963.

This cotton sateen utility uniform was converted for use by aggressor forces by wearing a green-and-white Circle Trigon Party patch on the pocket and the aggressor-style helmet liner, during 1st Inf Div exercise Gold Fire I at Fort Riley, Kansas, in August 1964.

Exercise Lava Plains Aggressor Forces Field Marshal Walker Heller negotiates armistice in May 1961. He wears distinguishing uniform composed by mixing army green uniform items with obsolete service breeches and legging-top boots.

The U.S. Army Aggressor Center at Fort Riley, Kansas, created a force trained and outfitted with Soviet-style uniforms and equipment, which eventually replaced aggressor uniforms by the end of the Vietnam War, to provide greater training realism.

which also added intelligence instruction during tactical training exercises. The U.S. Army Aggressor Center (TDA Organization 8215) at Fort Riley, Kansas, served as the supply agency for aggressor uniform items and equipment.

The authorized aggressor uniform was composed of unique helmet liners, tunics, and insignia. These could be supplemented by ordinary Army clothing modified to appear like "foreign enemy" attire. By the close of the Vietnam War, the Army began clothing and equipping a select aggressor unit in Soviet fashion instead.

The aggressor helmet was a helmet liner fitted with a curved wooden crest on top. A red garrison cap was worn by "elite" aggressor fusilier troops, and a black garrison cap was worn by tank and reconnaissance troops. Berets were worn by special-purpose troops. Generals and flag officers were encouraged to make distinguishing uniforms "from locally available material such as braid, sateen shoulder loops, sateen tabs, sateen stripes

on trousers, riding boots and breeches, swords and daggers."[15]

The jungle green Olive Drab shade 8 pullover tunic was another special aggressor uniform item. It was first made of 8.2-ounce cotton twill for summer, and 16-ounce wool for winter. Later a year-round tunic was made of 9-ounce cotton wind-resistant sateen. Different color tabs were worn on both sides of the collar, in conformity with the various branches of the aggressor forces. The Circle Trigon Party patch, a green triangle in a white circle, was worn on the upper left pocket.[16]

A complex uniform rank and unit identifying scheme was also put into effect, and entire manuals were devoted to their specifics. The first set of aggressor insignia included shoulder loops for officers and sleeve chevron-and-pip insignia for enlisted personnel. Later shoulder loops contained bars for enlisted troops, angled stripes for lower officers, combinations of stripes and bars for senior officers, and stripes and wreaths for generals.

The shoulder loops were red for fusilier officers, blue for airborne personnel, white for marshals and general officers, and green for all other aggressor personnel.

Protective Suits

During the Cold War the Army realized that its soldiers faced the immediate prospect of sustained operations within an atomic environment, but the need to satisfy cost-effective mass clothing production and individual comfort requirements hampered development of chemical-resistant combat attire. Soldiers were expected to fight in ordinary issue clothing and seek protection from nuclear detonations and radiation effects through such precautions as field entrenchment, riding in armored vehicles, and wearing improved masks.

The Army Quartermaster and Research Engineering Command researched and developed various types of experimental and limited-production protective clothing. The universal protective clothing ensemble was the practical culmination of these efforts during the Cold War era. This heat-regulated personal protective outfit was also known as thermalibrium clothing.

The ensemble was developed from a thermo-electric powered heating/ventilating system conceived by Westinghouse Electric Corporation and the Mine Safety Appliances Company in 1960. The key component was the air distribution garment, wherein both temperature and humidity were thermostatically controlled by mechanical air-conditioning and dehumidifying equipment linked to an integral power source within the clothing.

The complete thermalibrium clothing system consisted of a foundation garment known as the spacer system, an impermeable layer worn over the spacer system, and an outer suit. The distribution system was capable of delivering heat-regulated air into the ensemble at 12 cubic feet a minute, at a static water pressure of 4.6 inches. First successfully tested in 1963, using a low flow resistance, the system reportedly rendered the highest degree of air turbulence possible to give maximum evaporation cooling per unit air flow over the body surface. The total weight of the heat regulating system, not including fuel, was 10.35 pounds.[17]

Unfortunately, the universal protective cloth-

ing ensemble was functionally deficient because of its bulk and physical restrictions that limited normal movement and other routine soldiering tasks. As a result, these protective suits were restricted to technicians engaged in specialized tasks within the contact area. Continuing engineering design problems with the suit finally canceled its applicability to the atomic arena. Nevertheless, the ensemble's resistance to heat-induced hazards proved beneficial for Vietnam-era explosive ordnance disposal experts.

Army diving equipment was furnished by the

The universal protective clothing ensemble, with outfit partially uncovered by Lt. Emil Senkowski, showing its three thermalibrium clothing system layers during February 1963.

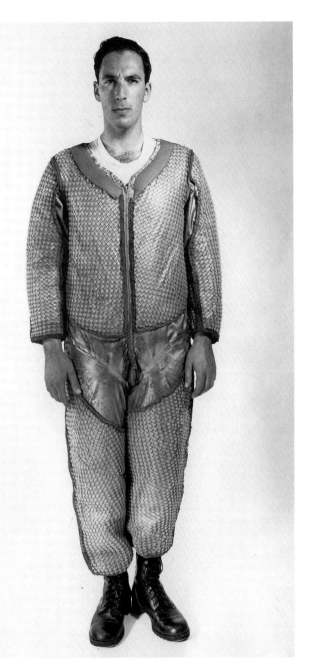 

Front and back views of the universal protective clothing ensemble's thermalibrium clothing spacer system. The impermeable layer worn over this spacer system, as well as an alternate outer layer for tropical conditions, is illustrated on p. 109 of *U.S. Army Uniforms of the Vietnam War.*

Corps of Engineers. For relatively light underwater work, divers used the Army diving equipment set for 1 Person at 30-foot depth, also termed the Light Aquatic Rebreathing Unit (LARU) diving set. It was a self-contained, closed-circuit oxygen swimming unit that could be supplemented by air hose and compressor. The outfit weighed 27 pounds, and its oxygen supply and carbon dioxide absorbent was sufficient for nearly two hours of underwater work.

The Toxilogical Agents Protective (TAP) suit worn by explosive ordnance disposal members, as shown by 41st Ordnance Detachment Pfc. Dester Haskins at Fort Bliss, Texas, in September 1968.

The Army diving equipment set for 2 Persons at 120-foot depth is placed on Army salvage diver Sp4 John Moran of the 20th General Support Group at the port of Inchon, Korea, during July 1969.

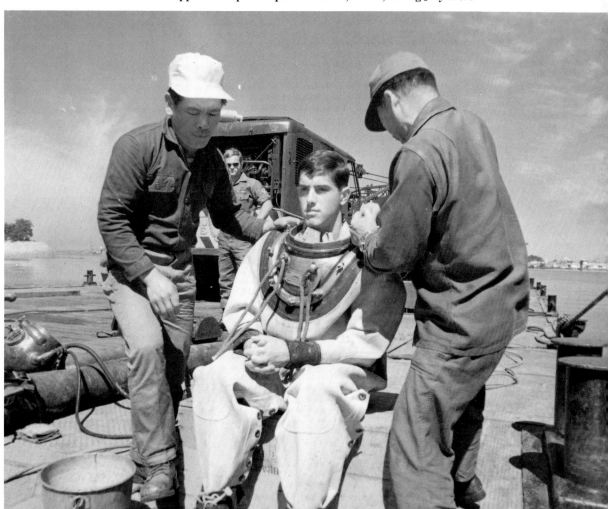

The copper deep-sea diver's helmet of the Army diving equipment set for 2 Persons at 120-foot depth. The diver's shoe with its brass toe plate is in the right foreground.

The LARU diver's dress was a three-piece rubberized cotton full-body swim suit. It was worn with diver's gloves, rubber swim fins or cotton duck gymnasium shoes, and molded rubber face mask. The mask had an aluminum frame and two eye cups, head harness straps, and a breathing valve assembly. The nylon vest assembly mounted the oxygen compressed-gas cylinder, regulator and automatic demand valves, horse-collar-shaped breathing bag, hose assembly, and carbon-dioxide absorbent canister. Other components included the cotton duck diver's belt, with pockets for inserting lead weights, wrist magnetic compass, depth gauge, watch, and a 6⅞-inch-long diver's knife with wood handle.[18]

For moderate underwater work, divers used the Army diving equipment set for 2 Persons at 100-foot depth. This equipment was designed for

tasks such as inspection and searching, clearing lines, and making minor underwater repairs. The 10-pound diver's dress was a one-piece full-body suit made of rubberized cotton drill and airplane cloth that opened at the back.

The suit was worn with a triangular diver's mask, which had a brass frame and plastic window, head harness, and air supply control valves. Reinforced diver's gloves and diver's trousers were also worn. The trousers were made of canvas duck with two tool pockets, knee patches, and four extension flaps that laced around the legs. The diver's shoes had corrugated-brass lower soles bolted to hard-maple upper soles, brass toe plates, and cotton duck tops. The shallow-water diver's belt was a 45-pound, chrome tanned-leather belt with leather shoulder and jock straps.[19]

For heavier underwater work, divers used the

Army diving equipment set for 2 Persons at 120-foot depth. This equipment was used for the construction and maintenance of port and harbor facilities and the clearing of obstructions. The diver's dress was a one-piece full-body suit, made of rubberized cotton drill, that opened at the collar and fitted to the copper deep-sea diver's helmet.

The helmet had a hinged front window, right and left side windows, regulating exhaust valve and telephone cable connections, and it attached to the lifeline and air hose. The diver also wore a felt-padded diver's helmet cushion, glove inserts with reinforced gloves, diver's trousers, and diver's shoes. The heavyweight diver's belt was an 84-pound, chrome tanned-leather belt with leather shoulder and jock straps.[20]

1. DA Circular 106, 27 October 1953.
2. MIL-J-3001B.
3. MIL-S-3001E.
4. MIL-S-3001F.
5. Natick Laboratories, *Clothing and Equipment Development Report No. 36,* February 1963.
6. DA Circular 670-1, 15 July 1963.
7. AR 670-5, Change 10, 29 August 1957.
8. DA Circular 670-22, 21 January 1958.
9. MIL-S-10858.
10. MIL-T-1870.
11. MIL-T-2060C and MIL-T-43497. Details of the M1951 field clothing are contained in the author's *U.S. Army Uniforms of the Korean War,* p. 49.
12. USARV Memorandum 670-1, 27 October 1967.
13. MIL-C-4399B. The tropical combat uniform is discussed in detail in the author's *U.S. Army Uniforms of the Vietnam War.*
14. Natick Laboratories, *Combined Infantry-Army Aviation Program Review: 1971,* Natick, Massachusetts, pp. 4, 49.
15. FM 30-101, Change 1, 27 April 1961.
16. FM 30-101, 27 April 1961.
17. Natick Laboratories universal protective clothing ensemble project task cards, commencing 1 January 1961.
18. DA Supply Manual 5-4-4220-S04, 9 November 1961.
19. DA Supply Manual 5-4-4220-S02, 3 November 1961.
20. DA Supply Manual 5-4-4220-S01, 3 November 1961.

10

Individual Equipment

Helmets

The Army provided the M1 helmet assembly to all soldiers, but tankers and aviators wore special helmets as required. The helmet assembly could be worn over the field cap, the field coat hood, or the insulating helmet liner. The assembly provided reasonably good protection against artillery and grenade fragments.

The World War II steel helmet, with the chin strap modifications accomplished by the end of the Korean War, remained essentially the same throughout the early Cold War period. The resin-impregnated cotton duck helmet liner had a head suspension system of webbing, to which was attached an adjustable head band, an adjustable neck band, and a leather chin strap.[1]

In 1964 a nylon resin-impregnated helmet liner, which gave additional ballistic protection, was introduced into the Army supply system. The internal web suspension system and head band were modified, and the neck band was replaced with a newer version that eliminated the need for the leather chin strap. Both models of the helmet liner had a version produced for parachutists that incorporated a special buckled chin strap.

Throughout this period DA conducted research and development on the helmet assembly, but nothing reached the troops. Two improved helmet liner suspensions had been tested by 1970. One featured a leather foam pad crown insert affixed to the helmet liner's removable suspension unit and a modified chin strap assembly. The second, known as the Welson-Davis suspension system, was a completely new Velcro-adjusted arrangement with sewn-in clips that were inserted into the mating studs of the helmet liner.

DA also developed experimental helmets during the Vietnam War to replace the M1 steel helmet assembly altogether. These test helmets included the LINCLOE nylon, LINCLOE titanium, and Type III titanium helmets. Extensive testing at Aberdeen Proving Ground during 1968 subjected the helmets to shell fragments from Type 42 high explosive 82mm mortar rounds and 120mm Chinese communist mortar rounds that were detonated 20–40 feet away. All the helmets stopped a significant percentage of the mortar shell splinters, but the titanium helmets afforded the best protection for the soldiers. The Army search for a new helmet was finally resolved with the adoption of the laminated Kevlar fabric Personnel Armament System Ground Troops (PASGT) helmet during 1978.[2]

M60 machine gunner of the 4th Armd Div at Grafenwoehr, Germany, has burlap-covered M1 steel helmet with field jacket hood during March 1964. His assistant gunner wears a helmet of World War II vintage with bar-tack chin strap instead of the clip-on feature. The soldier with a PRC-6 radio wears a burlap helmet cover.

The 1940-pattern cloth-covered fiber sun helmet, or "pith helmet," is worn with the utility uniform in Thailand during 1965. The sun helmet was supplied as required to SCARWAF units, amphibious engineers, and selected personnel in hot-climate regions.

Combat vehicle crewmen helmets worn by M60 tank crew of the 3d Bn, 70th Armor, 24th Inf Div, at Grafenwoehr, Germany, in 1964. The integral helmet headset and microphone permitted intercom and radio communication. The signal flag is used for control on the firing range.

M1 steel helmets are worn by a jeep patrol of the 1st Battle Group, 20th Inf, during Panama independence day demonstrations in November 1959. The driver has M9 special-purpose mask tucked into its open carrier, and M5 bayonet in M8A1 scabbard for M1 rifle. White bands are added on helmets for identification.

The M1 steel helmet combination is worn by soldier using the PPS-6 lightweight battlefield surveillance radar set at Fort Monmouth, New Jersey, during 1965. Note the clip-on attachment and quick-release device of the chin strap, which is secured along the back rim of helmet.

The LINCLOE prototype helmet, worn with gas mask, is being tested at Camp Pickett, Virginia, in August 1969. This was one of several experimental helmets made of nylon or titanium for increased battlefield protection that were evaluated during Vietnam era.

The Type A anti-riot plastic face shield, attached to the M1 helmet assembly with a spring band, was developed by the Army Natick Laboratories for Army personnel engaged in civil disturbance operations during the late 1960s.

The improved Type B anti-riot plastic face shield, with reinforced curvature and mounting device attached to spring band on M1 helmet, was available to troops opposing the anti-war demonstration in Washington in May 1971.

The protective helmet is worn with padded hand and groin protection during pugil stick training at the U.S. Army Training Center, Fort Bragg, North Carolina, in December 1969. Pugil sticks were used to teach aggressiveness in hand-to-hand combat as part of bayonet training.

Green berets are worn in typical fashion with utility uniforms by an 8th Special Forces Group mobile training team at the Peruvian Army Commando School at Canto Grande, Peru, during May 1963.

Sp4 Stephen Donovan wears the green beret with tropical combat uniform at the Jungle Warfare School, Fort Sherman, Panama Canal Zone, in January 1968. He wears the 8th Special Forces Group flash positioned on the beret's stiffened badge stay.

Patrol of the 8th Special Forces Group in Panama during 1963 wear green berets and camouflaged tropical hat. They carry (*front to rear*) TRC-77 receiver, transmitter, and battery accessory bag on the upper frames of their lightweight rucksacks. Note M1956 carrier and entrenching tool hooked on rucksack, and first-pattern tropical combat boots with buckled straps.

Soldiers with foliage secured in the helmet camouflage band board UH-19D "Chickasaw" helicopter for a field exercise in 1964. They carry M1945 combat field packs with M1943 entrenching tools, and have ponchos folded over the pistol belts. The radioman carries a PRC-10 radio.

Load-Carrying Suspenders and Belts

At the beginning of the Cold War era, soldiers carried equipment that was either direct or improved versions of the M1910 field equipment assembly that utilized double-hook fasteners. The infantryman still relied on specialized cartridge or magazine belts and field combat and field cargo packs, as supplemented by bandoleers, ammunition carrying bags, magazine pockets, and rocket carrying cases. The configuration and portage of these items are described and illustrated in previous volumes of this series.

After the Korean War DA embarked on a program to redesign the soldier's individual combat equipment completely. Although every attempt was made to reduce the load carried by the individual fighting man, the Army of the Cold War had to train for operations on a nuclear battlefield.

Greater dependency was placed on flexible gear that could accommodate mechanized or aerial transport and could be adjusted to carry various weapons and communication items.

The resulting M1956 system, which was adopted by QMCTC 3-57, allowed gear to be arranged on a reconfigured web pistol belt and field suspender combination. The exact equipment combination could be adjusted according to terrain, climate, and tactical conditions.[3]

The lightweight but sturdy load-carrying system gave better access and load balancing while retaining a minimum number of items. These items were general purpose in design and could meet a wider range of uses. The system also provided load carriage efficiency despite the bulk of clothing, and it offered more secure adjustments and closures that were easier to operate.

Furthermore, the system fulfilled the needs of

174

National Guard automatic rifleman of the 42d Inf Div with BAR carries M1945 combat field pack with rolled poncho strapped on top, M1943 entrenching shovel carrier, and M1937 BAR magazine belt as late as 1970 at Camp Drum, New York.

Troops of the 1st Battle Group, 23d Inf, are equipped for mountain operations at Fort Richardson, Alaska, in August 1962. They have burlap-covered helmets, mountain rucksacks, coiled climbing rope, crampons, M1950 heavy leather gloves, and ski-mountain boots.

Soldiers wearing the M1956 individual field equipment prepare to evacuate a wounded soldier. One soldier (*left*) wears the H-pattern field suspenders, M1961 field pack with poncho strapped underneath, and canteen cover attached on side. Soldier (*right*) has the sleeping bag carrier fastened to his suspenders.

Mortar crewmen of the 24th Inf Div in Germany prepare to fire their 81mm mortar. They wear the H-pattern M1956 field suspenders with ponchos folded over their individual equipment belts, alongside a canteen cover and M1916 holster for the .45-caliber pistol. Note plastic-top canteen, introduced in World War II.

marching order, when the soldier was acting as a porter and was out of contact with the enemy. It also met the needs of fighting order, when the soldier was carrying minimum essentials onto the battlefield. Finally, the system could be stripped to very light order when tasks such as night patrolling were undertaken. The system allowed the soldier to convert quickly from marching order into other modes without removing the entire equipment assembly.

The foundation of the M1956 load bearing system consisted of an adjustable individual equipment belt, to which all other equipment attached; field pack suspenders that connected to the belt and helped distribute the load weight over the shoulders; and compatible operational equipment

Section members of the 1st Bn, 34th Artillery, prepare to fire an Honest John rocket at Grafenwoehr, Germany, in 1964. They wear M1956 field suspenders and individual equipment belts with canteens, small arms ammunition cases, and M17 ABC field protective mask carriers. Note soldier checking elevation with the gunner's quadrant, with case suspended on his left side.

Paratroopers of the 101st Abn Div wear STABO extraction harness, and "Swiss-seat" rope arrangement for rappelling with M1950 heavy leather gloves attached to the snap links (carabiners). Note web chin straps of the M1 helmet assemblies for parachutists.

that fitted onto the harnesses. In addition, the universal load-carrying sling was a buckle-adjusted web strap that had side loops and snap fasteners for carrying other loads, such as mortar rounds or a water can.[4]

The individual equipment belt, a modified pistol belt, was made of cotton webbing in Olive Drab shade 7. The belt had a new black oxidized brass wire ball-type fastener and eyelets for the attachment of old-style M1910 double-hooked items of equipment. Newer M1956 family equipment components were fastened by attached interlocking slide keepers that clamped vertically on the belt.

The belt was produced in medium (27–44 inches) and long (35–56 inches) sizes. The soldier could further adjust the length to accommodate

different layers of clothing. Once a new size was determined, the belt was locked by hooking the end hooks into the nearest center eyelet, and further secured by its four sliding keepers.

The other basic component was the field pack suspenders. The web suspenders were made of cotton duck and wool felt in Olive Drab shade 7. The H-shape design consisted of two wide shoulder straps joined at the back and connected to a set of extension suspenders at each end.

The two front suspender extensions were hooked into the front of the individual equipment belt and adjusted for length with their clamp-style buckles. The shoulder straps were passed over the shoulders of the soldier, so that the padding was centered for even distribution of weight. The two rear suspender extensions were hooked either into

Soldiers of the 1st Bn, 3d Infantry, prepare to fire a 3.5-inch M20 rocket launcher during training in Virginia in June 1964. The gunner wears M1961 field pack, M1 bayonet in M7 scabbard attached to M1956 combination entrenching tool carrier, and M17 ABC field protective mask carrier.

the field pack or onto the rear of the individual equipment belt.

A sleeping bag carrier was provided for the transportation of bivouac equipment. This was an arrangement of straps of cotton webbing in Olive Drab shade 7. The two longest straps of the carrier buckled around the sleeping bag and held it in position. The two tie-down straps of the carrier were fitted with glove-type snap fasteners. The two attaching straps connected to the field pack suspenders for carrying purposes, and the "lift the dot" fasteners allowed quick release, in case the soldier needed to jettison the carrier and sleeping bag rapidly.

During the Vietnam era the Army also introduced pack adapter straps. The straps allowed the soldier to move the field pack higher on his back and away from the individual equipment belt, and thus prevent the pack's immersion in water. This was done in order to carry extra equipment on the individual equipment belt, or add heavier items like radios for back portage.[5]

In 1965 DA developed a new generation of lightweight load carrying equipment that was similar in design to the M1956 system, but made of nylon material and aluminum hardware instead of cotton and brass or steel. The nylon items were water resistant, retained less moisture, and dried faster. The details of these Vietnam-era M1967 components are described and illustrated in the author's *U.S. Army Uniforms of the Vietnam War* volume of this series.[6]

Crewmen of the 1st Armd Div being inspected at Fort Hood in March 1965 wear the M1956 sleeping bag carrier attached to their field suspenders by "lift the dot" snap fasteners. The M1956 field pack (*foreground*) contrasts with the M1961 field pack.

Vietnam-bound trainees enter a mock Viet Cong village at Fort Jackson, South Carolina, during 1968. Soldier in foreground wears M1956 field pack suspenders, canteen cover with plastic canteen, and M1961 field pack. Note the plastic window for insertion of owner's identification above the web handle of the field pack.

Field Packs and Other Equipment

The canvas field pack, or "butt pack," was made of hard-textured cotton duck in Olive Drab shade 7. It was designed to carry essential individual items such as rations, toilet articles, and mess gear, as well as miscellaneous items such as dry socks, which would be of immediate use to the soldier.

The first version of the field pack, termed the M1956, had a simple narrow flap and side extensions that folded over the contents. For better protection of the pack's contents, the M1961 version had an improved flap and a waterproof throat around the opening. The compact size of the 9x9-inch compartment could be expanded by raising the flap and adjusting the web strap buckles. Two bottom web straps were used to secure extra gear, such as a rolled poncho, underneath the pack.

The field pack had two interlocking slide keepers on the rear side for attachment to the individual equipment belt, and the pack could also be snapped to the field pack suspenders. The outside right edge of the flap contained a row of eyelets for the attachment of M1910 double-hooked fasten-

Army SWB sergeant wears an experimental arrangement of individual equipment to accommodate a bulky load in 1965. The M1956 field pack is attached to straps encompassing the pouches of the TRN-19 low frequency radio beacon transmitter and its two elongated antenna sections. Note M1942 first aid packet case used as a compass case and fastened to front of individual equipment belt.

An Army SWB soldier wears M1956 individual equipment to support AN/PRT-7 low frequency radio beacon case during 1965. He carries the M1956 field pack, small arms ammunition cases, and a canteen in prescribed arrangement.

ers. The pack could be hand-carried by a web handle on the flap, and a plastic identification window was located on the flap closure.

The universal small arms ammunition pouch, or later case, was made of cotton duck in Olive Drab shade 7. Each soldier carried two pouches on the belt in front. These were designed to carry a "universal" array of ammunition loads that the ordinary rifleman used. The soldier could carry two Browning automatic rifle (BAR) magazines, one folded bandoleer of six M1 rifle clips, or four 30-round carbine magazines. The pouch closed with a quick-release fastener, by putting a web tab

through a metal loop that was riveted to a billet sewn on the front.[7]

The box-type pouch attached to the individual equipment belt with two interlocking slide keepers. The pouch back supporting strap snapped to the front suspender extension and kept the pouch from hanging forward when loaded with ammunition. Plastic stiffeners were added for rigidity of the pouch. Snap-closed web straps on each side of the pouch secured the hand grenades that could be fitted into the pouch side slots.

The field first aid dressing–magnetic compass case (either item could be carried inside) was made

184

of cotton duck in Olive Drab shade 7. The small case closed by means of a snap-closed fastener and was attached to the individual equipment belt by an interlocking slide keeper.

The canteen cover was made of cotton duck in Olive Drab shade 7, and lined with gray wool felt. The cover attached to the individual equipment belt on the right side with two interlocking slide keepers. The one-quart aluminum or stainless steel canteen fitted into a canteen cup with its handle folded down, and both were placed inside the canteen cover. A polyethylene (plastic) canteen gradually replaced the older metal canteens during the 1960s.

The intrenching tool carrier was made of cotton duck material in Olive Drab shade 7. The carrier attached to the individual equipment belt on the left side with two interlocking slide keepers on the rear. Leather reinforcements on the front of the carrier were provided with a web equipment tab to receive the double-hook fasteners of the bayonet or bayonet knife scabbard. A web strap secured the bayonet scabbard from movement.[8]

This carrier was used to transport the hand-combination intrenching tool, which was a modified version of the M1943 intrenching shovel. The tool was carried in collapsed position with its pick and shovel blades folded down on the hickory handle. The blades were unfolded to desired working angles by adjusting the tool lock-nut.

During the Cold War era, the Army emphasized development of products suitable for fighting the Soviet military in a European winter environment. Typical of this development was the cold-weather insulated one-quart canteen. It was vacuum insulated and had a round stainless steel body with polyethylene cap and a silicone rubber mouthpiece. The canteen, when filled with water and assembled with its compatible half-shell cup, cover, and closure, weighed about 4 pounds. Water, when placed in the canteen at a temperature of 50 degrees Fahrenheit, was kept in a fluid state at outside air temperatures down to minus 40 degrees Fahrenheit for six hours. When placed in the canteen at a temperature of 180 degrees Fahrenheit, water dropped no more than 40 degrees when the canteen was placed in outside air at a temperature of minus 40 degrees Fahrenheit for six hours.[9]

The Army also continued to develop equipment to protect the soldier under the chemical-biological-radiological conditions that were expected on a European battlefield. The M9 special-purpose

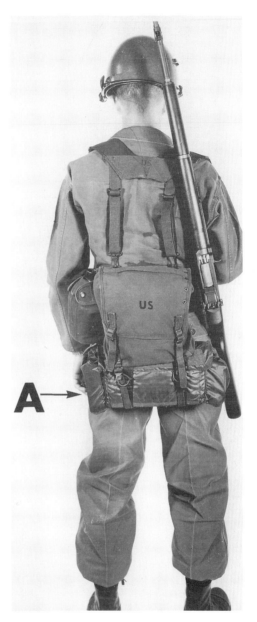

Soldier straps PRC-64 radio set in its carrying case (A) beneath the M1956 field pack during 1964. The case held the radio transmitter, and its side pouches held doublet antenna reels and a spare battery. Note the canteen worn on the left side.

185

Field portage of some items required two soldiers. Seventh Army radio/telephone operator (*left*) carries the 1960-pattern NATO tactical radio (a French high-frequency single-sideband tactical radio set) and his assistant carries the set's nickel-cadmium battery pack.

mask had a canister attached to the facepiece on either the right or left cheek position. The M9 gave protection to the wearer's face, eyes, and respiratory tract against some chemical and biological agents. The mask was deficient, however, and it was replaced by the M17 Army biological-chemical (ABC) field protective mask.

The M17 ABC field protective mask provided protection from some toxic chemical agents, and was used to protect the face, eyes, and respiratory tract of the wearer from field concentrations of chemical and biological agents. It did not protect the user against ammonia or carbon monoxide, and it failed to function in confined areas with

M1956 (first-pattern) canvas field pack.

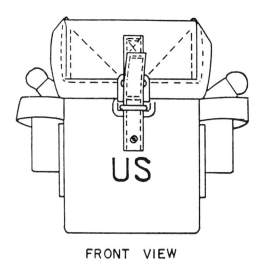

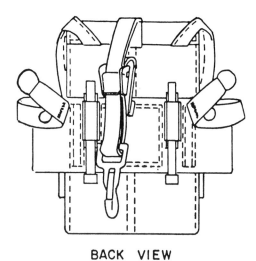

FRONT VIEW   BACK VIEW

Universal small arms ammunition pouch. Note the two interlocking slide keepers centered on the back of the pouch.

Paratroopers of the 82d Abn Div wear M17 ABC field protective masks during anti-riot training at Fort Bragg, North Carolina, in 1968. The mask carriers are worn in the thigh-carry position commonly used during riot situations.

Soldiers of the 91st Engineer Bn wear M17 ABC field protective masks, which contrast with the M9 special-purpose mask of the police officer while deployed in Washington, D.C., in 1968, during civil disturbance operations. Note .45-caliber magazine double-web pocket (*right*).

an atmospheric oxygen content below 18 percent. The mask also failed when wet.

The M17 mask consisted of a facepiece with either an integral or connector system for filtering toxic agents from inspired air. The mask had dual lenses with the filter system mounted on or within the facepiece. The M17A1 version included a water drinking and resuscitation device. Both these masks were placed in Olive Drab shade 7 cotton duck carriers that were fastened to the soldier by web straps in prescribed fashion, such as the common thigh-carry position.

Identification tags were worn by the soldier at all times when in the field, when in garrison, while

traveling in aircraft, or whenever outside the continental United States. One identification tag was suspended from the neck, underneath the clothing, by a 25-inch non-corrosive necklace. The second identification tag was fastened to the necklace below the first tag by a necklace extension.

Parachutists Equipment

Army parachutists used the T-10 parachute assembly, which consisted of a backpack-carried main parachute that deployed automatically by means of a static line; a parachute harness with a saddle

The method of wearing the T-10 parachute assembly with equipment inside the aviator's kit bag, beneath reserve parachute (*left*), can be compared to the pre-1963 exterior method of wearing individual jumping equipment with entrenching tool handle secured by a cord tied down to the leg.

The M1950 parachutist's adjustable individual weapons case was secured vertically by a quick-release strap attached to the left D-ring on the T-10 parachute harness. Paratroopers board C-130 aircraft for a night jump over Fort Greely, Alaska, during 1968.

Paratroopers jumped with individual equipment and sleeping bags inside the aviator's kit bag, secured by H-harness beneath the reserve parachute. During 1963 the T-10 parachute harness was fitted with quick-release assemblies on each shoulder, which allowed the jumper to disengage the canopy upon landing.

190

Sp4 Johnson wears parachutist crash helmet with parachutist's adjustable equipment bag rigged to jump the TRN-20 low frequency radio beacon. The bag, carried below the reserve parachute, was attached to the main harness by a 20-foot lowering strap.

and straps around the chest, legs, and back; and a reserve parachute, hand-activated with a rip-cord handle. During 1962, following a series of mishaps caused by wind gusts dragging para-troopers across the ground, a quick-release system was added to the assembly. This allowed soldiers a rapid means of disconnecting the main canopy upon landing.

The High Altitude, Low Opening (HALO)

parachute assembly was part of a free-fall, delay-opening parachute system that enabled the Army to deliver personnel and their equipment secretly into small and relatively inaccessible drop zones. The parachutist descended using body stabiliza-tion techniques, until a pressure-sensing device automatically activated the steerable parachute at a predetermined altitude. The assembly consisted of a HALO parachute, a T-10 reserve parachute,

Members of the Army "Golden Knights" Parachute Team use the free-fall, steerable HALO parachute assembly during a jump in July 1970. Note altimeter and stopwatch mounted on instrument panel, which was hooked to the parachute harness D-rings (*right*).

During 1964 HALO equipment consisted of the MB-3A protective flying helmet, goggles and oxygen mask, HALO parachute harness assembly, altimeter and stopwatch on instrument panel, T-10 reserve parachute, and T-59 parachutist equipment container. Sergeants check canopy releases and riser locking forks.

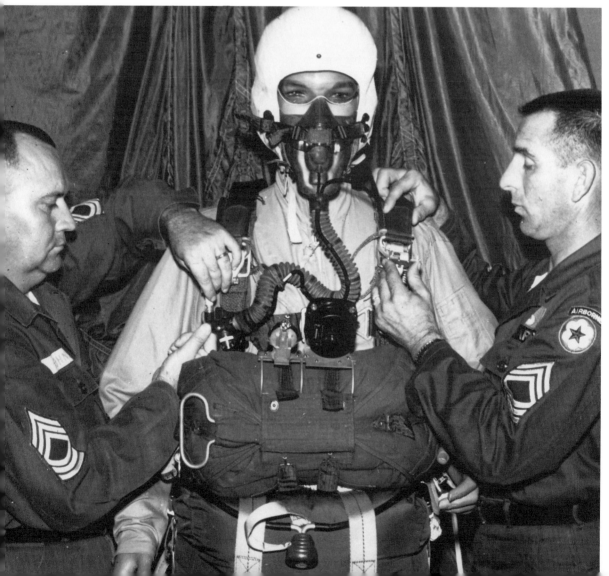

MB-3A protective flying helmet with goggles, oxygen mask, panel-mounted altimeter and stopwatch, aviator's kit bag, T-59 parachutist (HALO) equipment container, .45-caliber pistol with shoulder holster, and knife.[10]

1. DA OQMG Adopted Items of Material, 30 January 1954.
2. Natick Laboratories, *Research and Development Command Fact Sheet,* April 1981.
3. SB 10-509, 1 August 1960.
4. FM 21-15, 24 August 1961.
5. FM 21-15, 6 January 1966.
6. FM 21-15, 28 August 1972, and the author's *U.S. Army Uniforms of the Vietnam War,* p. 145.
7. TB QM-107, 8 July 1960.
8. TB QM-73, April 1957.
9. MIL-C-43761, 29 November 1971.
10. TM 57-220, 24 January 1965 and 4 June 1968.

11

Women's Uniforms

Taupe and Beige Uniforms

The Army uniform board of 1949 recommended a distinct and harmonious uniform system for all personnel of the Women's Army Corps, Army Nurse Corps, and the Women's Medical Specialist Corps (later Army Medical Department women) with the exception of special duty items, such as the nurses' white hospital duty uniforms. This new fashionable ensemble of wool serge and cotton taupe uniforms, which had replaced the olive drab uniforms of World War II, served the purpose of general duty and semi-dress uniforms for winter and summer wear.[1]

The Army had concentrated its development and production efforts on the problems of providing distinctive female clothing, in contrast to the emphasis on durability and functional color requirements for men's clothing. DA wanted uniforms with "attractive feminine styling" for its female soldiers, and catered to figure variation by allowing more highly flared, sheathed, or tailored design features. DA also insisted on a distinctive identifying color scheme for women's uniforms that, unlike male uniform considerations, emphasized compatibility with the color of accessories.

The Army introduced a summer semi-dress uniform on 13 May 1954, which was originally termed the light taupe suit, but later designated as the beige uniform. It was made of 10.5-ounce tropical worsted or 11-ounce wool gabardine in light Beige shade 146, and known informally as the "silver taupe" uniform. The well-liked optional uniform rapidly gained acceptance as the uniform of choice, and during 1962 it became mandatory for officer purchase. The beige uniform remained in Army inventory until 1 July 1968.[2]

The beige uniform included a garrison cap and service hat of the same design that was introduced in 1952 with the taupe uniform, a coat, and a skirt. The coat was first produced with bronze buttons. Effective 1 January 1961 the Army commenced the changeover to gold-colored buttons, which was completed by 1 January 1963. Officer sleeve ornamentation consisted of ½-inch-wide Light Taupe shade 145 braid on the cuff.[3]

The beige uniform skirt was worn with cotton shirtwaist in Tan shade 130 and detachable brown neck tab. Other uniform items included the cotton/nylon gloves in Gray-Beige shade 270, and cafe brown service handbag and matching oxfords or optional calfskin pumps. During the 1960s the

Enlisted women of the Army, Marine Corps, Navy, and Air Force model comparable uniforms during February 1956. The Army master sergeant (*left*) wears the standard taupe wool semi-dress uniform. Note the one-sided brim of the hat and its compensating angle of wear.

Members of the WAC Detachment, 7th Signal Service Bn, wear wool serge taupe uniforms and wool taupe caps in Paris during April 1953. The fashionable "Doir New Look" styling of the skirt is evident.

Members of the 3440th Army Unit (WAC Detachment) at Fort Benning, Georgia, wear taupe uniforms in formation during May 1953. Some of the women have cafe brown leather gloves. Note the positioning of the garrison-style wool taupe caps.

Senior WAC officers wear the beige summer uniform, which can be compared with the tropical worsted uniform of Lt. Gen. Carter Magruder, at the Pentagon during September 1957. Note that two officers wear the DA General Staff Identification Badge on the right sides of their coats.

uniform was also produced in two lightweight blended fabrics, 9-ounce polyester/wool tropical and 9.5-ounce polyester/wool gabardine.

Green and Green Cord Uniforms

The introduction of the army green uniform for male personnel, coupled with the increasing complaints about the taupe uniform, led to the 1956 uniform board decision to proceed with the development of a green uniform system for Army women. In the meantime, the accessories for the new green uniform gradually began to replace the

cafe brown leather items of the taupe uniform, which was completed by August 1962.[4]

On 1 July 1960 the Army switched to black footwear for all female uniforms, by the simple expedient of issuing dye kits from the Fort Mc-Clellan clothing point. On the same date the changeover began from enlisted chamois insignia of grade on a taupe background to goldenlite on a green background. A one-year phaseout allowed the former chevrons to be worn until 1 July 1961. These accessory changes were carried out as the new green uniforms were being introduced.

The first of the new green uniforms was the summer green cord uniform, authorized for wear

(*Above*) Lt. Joan Shetierly of the WAC Detachment, Oakland Army Terminal in California, wears a beige uniform with green hat, which can be compared to the standard army khaki uniform with garrison cap (*left*) and the army tan uniform with service cap (*right*) during June 1964.

(*Left*) The enlisted beige uniform is displayed by Pfc. Dorothy McSwain in June 1963, after the transition to green uniform accessories, such as the green hat and black neck tab. Note fashionable tightness of the uniform and optional commercial pumps.

(*Right*) The green cord uniform is worn by a lieutenant of the Army Nurse Corps at the Pentagon in May 1965. Note officers' gold braid on hat, black service handbag, and gray-beige gloves. Optional commercial pumps are worn.

Medical personnel of the 97th General Hospital in Frankfurt, Germany, wear the green cord uniform with garrison cap during September 1960.

beginning on 1 March 1959. The green cord uniform, adopted by QMCTC 2-59, represented the classic 1950s penchant for cord weave fabric, which possessed more body and wrinkle-resistance than plain weave flat fabrics. The uniform was made of 4.3-ounce polyester and cotton cord fabric in Army Green shade 160. It became the official summer duty uniform effective 1 March 1961.[5]

The single-breasted, short-sleeve coat had a four-button front closure, shoulder loops, and slanted hip pockets. The rounded collar and cuffs were trimmed with polyester cord-edge braid in dark Army Green shade 260. The buttons were originally bronze. On 1 July 1964 gold buttons were introduced, and the changeover was completed by 1 April 1964.[6]

(*Above*) Chief nurse Col. Mercedes Fischer wears the green cord uniform while being decorated with the Legion of Merit at Fort Shafter, Hawaii, during June 1971. Note U.S. and branch insignia on collars, and rank and distinctive unit insignia on shoulder.

(*Left*) Medical specialist Sp4 Vera Sescat wears the green cord uniform at Fort MacArthur, California, in April 1962. Her sitting posture shows the snug fit of the coat. Note the dark green cord-edge braid on collar and cuffs.

(*Right*) The green cord uniform of Lt. Patricia Thomas (*center*) contrasts with the green uniform of Army Medical Specialist Corps chief Col. June Williams at Fort Wolters, Texas, during April 1971. Note white cotton hospital coat and tan uniform.

(*Left*) **Capt. Zetta Jones wears the first-pattern green uniform in June 1957, with black handbag and gloves, in Washington, D.C. This rare photograph shows the original-model green hat with upward curving semi-brim that was styled like the taupe hat.**

The six-gore skirt had a concealed slide fastener at the left side and a sewn-on waistband with a single-button closure. Army fitting instructions stated, "In order to present a narrow and trim silhouette, the skirt should fit snugly over the hips so that it does not drape in folds and so that the loose hipline of the coat is accentuated. The skirt length is established according to the wearer's height." With the popularity of civilian fashion extremes, skirts were actually shortened according to individual judgment, challenging DA-regulated lengths.[7]

Headgear originally consisted of the green cord garrison cap, which was approved in December 1959. It was designed in close-fitting style, with double outside curtains and crown lining, and was trimmed in dark green cord-edge braid. Other uniform accessories included an acrylic rayon scarf in Gray-Beige shade 273, black service handbag, gray-beige gloves or white gloves worn on ceremonial occasions as prescribed, knitted wool Taupe shade 59 cardigan sweater, and issue black oxfords or optional pumps.

The green uniform was approved in 1957 for officer purchase, and issue of the uniform to enlisted women began on 1 July 1960. The green uniform was declared the women's winter duty uniform for all ranks on 1 October 1962. It consisted of the green hat or garrison cap, green coat, and green skirt.

Army fitting instructions for the green uniform stressed feminine styling: "The uniform is designed to fit the figure easily with smooth tailored lines. The lines of the coat are soft with lightly padded shoulders, rounded hipline, and slightly suppressed waist. The skirt, viewed from

(*Right*) **Army Nurse Corps lieutenant wears the green uniform at the Pentagon in May 1968. The standard green hat brim formed a high cuff across the back and was rolled on both sides to make a short straight visor in front.**

Lt. Martha Monroe wears the green uniform during promotion ceremonies at Fort Sam Houston, Texas, during 1968. Her green coat is worn with tan shirt and neck tab. Note the slanted front hip pockets, name plate, and black mohair braid on lower sleeves.

The men's and women's green uniforms, worn with appropriate service caps, are contrasted at the Presidio of San Francisco during April 1968. The introduction of lightweight polyester/wool fabrics expanded green uniform wear to a year-round basis.

The green uniform is worn by WAC receptionist and senior aide at the entrance to the Army COFS office at the Pentagon during May 1970. The skirt is worn in fashionable length. Note the gold-colored service aiguillette worn on left shoulder of aide.

back or front, should continue the slender lines of the coat without flaring at the sides."[8]

The green uniform was initially made of 12-, 14-, or 15-ounce wool serge or 11-ounce wool gabardine in Army Green shade 44. On 20 May 1966 a lightweight green uniform version was produced in Army Green shade 344, using blended lightweight 9-ounce polyester/tropical wool or 9.5-ounce polyester/wool in gabardine weave. The choice of material gave the uniform more suitability for wear on a year-round basis.[9]

WAC Pfc. Muriel Ferguson wears the green uniform while performing stenographer duties at the office of the Fort Sheridan post commandant in April 1962. Plain pumps of suitable commercial design were purchased with the enlisted clothing allowance.

The first Army women generals, Brig. Gen. Elizabeth Hoisington and Anna Hays, board an aircraft in Chicago during June 1970. Their aides carry accessories. Note the rolled-brim design of the green hat and ornamentation of gold bullion laurel leaves for senior officers.

The Medical Field Service School staff and newly graduated nurses at Fort Sam Houston, Texas, wear green uniforms during 1968. The men's uniforms are compatible, except that black gloves are lacking. Note mix of low-quarter oxford shoes and pumps.

The hip-length, single-breasted coat had an open collar with rounded ends, shoulder loops, slanted front hip pockets with simulated slot seams, and a four-button front. Officer coat ornamentation consisted of ½-inch-wide black ribbed mohair on the cuff. The six-gore skirt had a sewn-on waistband with a two-button closure on the left side and a concealed slide-fastened closure.

The shirt worn with the green uniform was initially a long- or short-sleeve shirt in Tan shade 130 with detachable black neck tab. This shirt was replaced by the polyester/cotton short-sleeve shirt in Tan shade 446 during the fall of 1967. The hip-length shirt had a six-button front closure and short cuffed sleeves. During 1972 the white shirt was permitted for wear with the green uniform. Shirt collars were worn closed at all times, and the shirt

was not worn as an outer garment except in the immediate workplace.[10]

The green hat in Army Green shade 44 was introduced on 20 October 1959 as optional headgear. The first green hat was the same pattern as the taupe-pattern hat, with tilted brim, but the insignia was placed symmetrically instead of the off-center positioning on the taupe hat. A new-style green hat was first announced in DA regulations on 3 April 1962, but it was not available for issue to enlisted women until 1 January 1964. At that time the taupe hat was officially replaced. The green hat had a reinforced crown, and its wool serge brim formed a high cuff across the back that rolled on both sides and formed a short flat visor.[11]

The standard green hat's detachable hat band had three rows of top stitching and an oval rise in

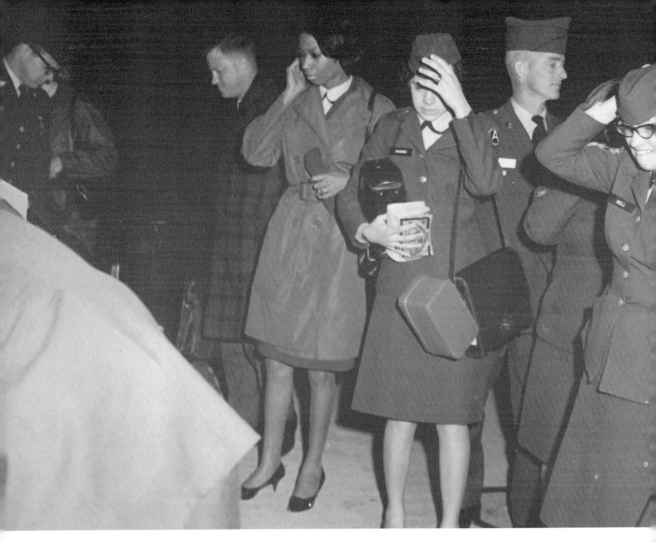

WAC soldiers from Fort Bragg are positioned near the Pentagon in preparation for the 21 October 1967 anti-war demonstration. The absence of equipment belts forced WACs to carry necessary items in handbags and portable cases. Note raincoat hem above skirt.

An MP of the 561st MP Company at Fort Myer, Virginia, wears the new green pantsuit during 1974. The uniform was supplied first to women assigned military police duties, but it was not adopted for Army-wide issue until 1976.

front, for centering of the gold-colored cap insignia that replaced the former antiqued brass hat insignia. Green hats for company-grade and warrant officers (captains and below) had ½-inch gold braid superimposed on the bottom edge of the hat band, while hats for senior officers (field grade and above) featured ornamentation of gold bullion laurel leaves.

Other uniform accessories included a small black service handbag, adopted from the Navy, and replaced in 1969 by the reintroduction of the Army handbag because of its larger pocket space. The gray-beige scarf could be worn. Gray-beige gloves or black leather gloves were also available for seasonal wear. Footwear consisted of black oxfords or pumps.

The initial standard-issue raincoat for the taupe ensemble with removable hood was made in nylon/rayon Taupe shade 121. This garment proved unsatisfactory and a commercial-variant tan opaque vinyl-film raincoat was authorized effective 12 May 1960. The cotton/nylon raincoat in Army Green shade 274, with removable visored havelock, was finally issued during 1966. The two earlier raincoat types were declared obsolete in July 1968.[12]

The overcoat was initially made of wool serge or wool gabardine in Taupe shade 121 and had a removable liner. During 1967 it was replaced by the wool gabardine green overcoat in Army Green shade 44. The full-length, double-breasted overcoat had buttoned-down shoulder loops, a convertible rounded collar, welt-type vertical pockets on each front, and a buttoned-in liner that could be removed for wear with the green raincoat.

Blue and White Uniforms

The blue uniform was introduced on 13 June 1957, when it was authorized for attendance at official or state functions or ceremonies, and during social occasions after retreat. The "dress blues" uniform, as it was known by service members, was mandatory for officers and warrant officers and optional for enlisted personnel. It consisted of a blue hat, blue coat, white shirt with black neck tab, and blue skirt.[13]

The blue uniform was made of a selection of material to provide individual suitability and year-round comfort. It was made of 12- or 14-ounce wool barathea, 16-ounce wool elastique, 11 or

Green cord uniform, shown for enlisted WAC, with skirt shortened to 1969 fashion length.

The blue uniform is worn by Maj. Lillian Baker at Cameron Station, Virginia, in June 1963. The 1962-pattern blue hat, under glove at left, had comparable green hat styling and replaced the former blue hat with turned-down brim.

Army Nurse Corps Lt. Col. Aloha Hammerly wears the blue uniform at the Pentagon in December 1964. The shoulder strap was curved to fit the shoulder. It had a gold-bordered field in branch-of-service coloration (in this case, maroon piped-in white for Army Medical Department) and embroidered insignia of grade.

14.5-ounce wool gabardine, and 10.5-ounce wool tropical in Blue shade 150. Commencing in the 1960s, a lightweight blue uniform in Blue shade 450 was produced from 9-ounce polyester/tropical wool and 9.5-ounce polyester/wool in gabardine weave.[14]

The first blue hat featured a turned-down brim like that of the taupe hat. On 5 July 1962 a new blue hat was introduced. It was designed like the green hat, with a brim that molded into a high back, rolled sides, and straight visor front. The older model blue hat became obsolete on 30 June 1969.[15]

The officer blue coat contained integral

shoulder loops until 1 October 1960, when shoulder straps were approved. The straps were bordered in gold trim, with embroidered insignia of grade on a background that was in the color of branch-of-service. A second color formed an inner border if the branch was authorized one (such as a maroon field with a white inner border for the Army Medical Department). Officer sleeve ornamentation consisted of ¾-inch gold-trimmed braid in branch-of-service coloration. Enlisted coat ornamentation consisted of shoulder loops, piped-in gold braid, and narrow ⅛-inch gold braid on the cuff.[16]

The blue uniform was worn with the short blue cape, designated as the Type I blue cape effective 20 October 1959. The Blue shade 150 cape was made of wool barathea, wool elastique, wool gabardine, wool tropical, or blended wool/polyester fabrics. The cape lining was rayon twill or satin in the first color of branch-of-service: maroon for Army Medical Department, old gold for Women's Army Corps, and brown for warrant officers. The finger-length cape had fitted shoulders and a high rounded soft collar with reversed tab ends. Other uniform items included white scarf for the optional taupe wool overcoat, black dress

Blue uniforms, green uniforms, and white cotton hospital duty uniforms with cap and knit sweater are worn by Army Nurse Corps officers at Martin Army Hospital, Fort Benning, Georgia, during February 1967.

The different white uniforms for men and women are shown during a WAC review parade at Fort McClellan, Alabama, in June 1968. Lt. Col. Tran Cam Huong (*second from left*) wears the uniform of the South Vietnamese women's armed forces corps.

handbag or a black service handbag for duty hours only, white dress gloves, and black pumps.

The white uniform served as optional attire for attendance at official or social occasions where formal summer dress attire was appropriate. The uniform, however, was mandatory for certain officers serving in tropical or semi-tropical regions outside the continental United States.

The first-pattern, closed-collar white dress uniform was adopted as part of the uniform ensemble created by fashion designer Hattie Carnegie. On 20 October 1959 a new white uniform, with the open collar design of the beige uniform, was authorized. It was commonly made of 6- or 8-ounce white polyester/rayon or gabardine. In 1962 the white hat was restyled to conform to the design of the green hat.[17]

White uniform coat ornamentation for officers and warrant officers consisted of ½-inch white braid on the cuffs. A white shirt was worn with black neck tab, along with the white skirt. Other white uniform accessories included white dress gloves and plain untrimmed white pumps of commercial design.

WAC Director Col. Mary Rasmuson wears the 1959-pattern white uniform, optional for officers and warrant officers attending stateside summer formalities, at a reception at Fort Myer, Virginia, during May 1962. Note medals worn on coat.

Blue uniform as worn in 1962, shown for WAC major, when the new-style blue hat was introduced. Hat ornamentation contains gold bullion laurel leaves for field grade officer.

Evening and Mess Uniforms

On 16 September 1952 an optional evening dress uniform was authorized for officers attending social functions and private dinners where formal attire was appropriate. The uniform was made of lustrous woolen 10.5-ounce broadcloth in Midnight Blue shade 176 with blue suede accessories. Unfortunately, it was too expensive for most officers and the blue uniform later offered a more affordable alternative. As a result, the evening dress uniform was rarely worn.[18]

The blue headband, or "tiara," featured embroidered gold bullion laurel leaves, and was worn centered on the head in coronet fashion. The "princess-style" evening jacket had collar trimming of gold bullion embroidered laurel leaves, and sleeve insignia of grade in a gold-colored design of trefoil and horizontal braid on a midnight blue broadcloth background. A white silk crepe blouse and floor-length evening skirt were also worn. A cummerbund of silk faille or rayon twill in Midnight Blue shade 196 was optional.

The evening dress uniform was worn with a blue cape, made of wool broadcloth in Midnight Blue shade 176 with a gold-colored lining in Gold shade 145. On 13 June 1957 the rayon twill or satin lining was changed to Old Gold shade 175. The cape was different from the blue uniform cape because of its length and, effective 20 October 1959, the addition of gold-bordered dark blue shoulder straps containing embroidered insignia of grade. As a result, it was designated the Type II blue cape.[19]

Other evening dress uniform accessories included white evening gloves, made of kid or doeskin, and the blue evening handbag. The evening blue pumps were plain opera pumps of commercial design in suede or silk fabric.

On 13 May 1969 the Army Uniform Board approved five evening uniforms on an optional basis, which gave a wider practical and more modern range of ensembles for formal functions and social events demanding proper attire. In addition, mess jackets and skirts could be interchanged with accessories to fit the occasion with the most appropriate uniform. The Type II cape exterior color was changed to black.

The officer's black mess uniform was composed of a black jacket in 8.5-ounce tropical wool or 9-ounce polyester/tropical wool. The "street-

The black evening dress uniform is worn at Fort McClellan, Alabama. It was authorized for optional wear by officers and warrant officers on a year-round basis for formal social occasions of an official or private nature. Note blouse design.

Officer in the all-white mess uniform, consisting of white jacket, street-length white skirt, white cummerbund, black neck tab, and white accessories.

215

Evening dress uniform adopted in 1952, shown for WAC colonel, with and without cape.

Evening mess dress uniform, shown for WAC officer, adopted in 1969.

length skirt," as defined by AR 670-30, was made of the same material. The uniform was worn with white blouse, black dress neck tab, and optional black cummerbund. Jacket ornamentation consisted of ½-inch-wide mohair braid on the cuff, and detachable shoulder boards.

The officers' white mess uniform consisted of a white jacket in 6- or 8-ounce polyester/rayon fabric with gabardine weave, a black street-length skirt, white blouse with black dress neck tab, and black cummerbund. The officers' all-white mess uniform was composed of a white jacket, street-length white skirt, white blouse with black dress neck tab, white cummerbund, and white accessories.

The black evening dress and white evening dress uniforms officially replaced the evening dress uniform adopted in 1952. The new dress uniforms consisted of either a black or white mess jacket, white blouse with dress neck tab and black cummerbund, and a black floor-length skirt. The matching accessories corresponded to the color of the dress uniform being worn.

Field and Work Clothing

The World War II–era two-piece hot-weather field/work uniforms consisted of either olive drab HBT or khaki poplin shirt and slacks. The latter was phased out in 1954, but HBT work attire continued to be used until 1969 for training, field, and maintenance duties. The shirt and slacks were made of 8.5-ounce herringbone twill in Olive Drab shade 7. The shirt could be worn tucked inside the slacks or as an outer garment with its collar open or closed. The sleeves were not normally rolled up.

The HBT shirt had five buttons and a protective fly-piece on the front, two patch pockets with buttoned flaps, a yoke back, and long sleeves with one-button adjustments. The HBT slacks were designed with a one-piece waistband with side button adjustments, two side openings with protective gusset pieces, two front patch pockets with slanted tops and buttoned flaps, and ankle adjustment tabs.

The Army program to develop new field clothing experienced numerous delays. With the increased role of female personnel in field exercises, there was a need for a modern field work uniform. During 1962 the Quartermaster Field

WAC Warrant Officer Jannace Van Tuyl, photo intelligence expert with the Eighth Army imagery interpretation center, at the Korean demilitarized zone (DMZ) in June 1964. She wears blocked cap, olive drab utility shirt, cotton sateen slacks, and low-quarter shoes.

Evaluation Agency conducted extensive testing of cotton poplin field outfits, but these proved unsatisfactory. Necessary modifications were expedited because of the Vietnam-generated expansion of the WAC and Army Nurse Corps. During 1964, following the conclusion of further testing at the Brooke Army Medical Center, the new hot-weather uniform was type-classified for interim wear in Southeast Asia.

On 5 October 1966 DA began standard issue of this uniform, which consisted of Olive Green shade 107 cotton poplin field shirt and slacks and service boots. It was known informally as "women's combat fatigues" because of Vietnam battle-

A nurse tests the experimental hot-weather field uniform while working in a mobile Army surgical hospital at Fort Sam Houston, Texas, during 1963. The Quartermaster Field Evaluation Agency played a key role in developing the OG-107 cotton poplin outfit.

Capt. Nellie Harness wears the hot-weather field uniform at the Walter Reed Army Medical Center in Washington, D.C., during April 1969. The shirt was normally worn with sleeves rolled up, and in coat-style over the trousers. Note tropical combat boots.

The 1969-pattern winter field clothing in Olive Green shade 108 could be worn with field coat, tan shirt with neck tab, and field skirt. An alternate outfit was composed of the wool flannel shirt worn in coat fashion with the field slacks.

The green raincoat is worn by an officer at the Pentagon during May 1968. The cotton/nylon raincoat in Army Green shade 274 also had a removable visored havelock.

field employment. Headgear included the tropical combat hat (confined to Southeast Asia) and the utility cap, which was identical to that used by male soldiers. Footwear consisted of black low-quarter oxfords and brown high-quarter service shoes. During 1963 black leather service boots, which were the female equivalent of the combat boot, were introduced as organizational equipment.[20]

The hot-weather field shirt was single-breasted with side vents and had two breast patch pockets with buttoned flaps and a patch pocket on the left sleeve. The shirt also had buttoned shoulder loops, a convertible collar, a five-button front with anti-exposure protective flap, and sleeves with buttoned strap closures. The hot-weather field slacks were slightly tapered. They had two front bellows-type pockets with buttoned flaps, front and back waistbands with adjusting tabs, and a two-button protective gusset closure at each side.

The World War II–era winter field uniform was composed of a cotton coat, wool shirt, and slacks. The five-button coat was made of wind-resistant and water-repellent 9-ounce cotton sateen cloth in Olive Drab shade 7, and lined with 5-ounce cotton poplin. The coat had convertible collar and lapels, two dummy upper pockets and two lower inside-hanging pockets with concealed-button flaps, and buttoned cuffs. The slacks had a separate waistband that buttoned at the left side, a right side pocket, and a placket opening with two-button closure on the left side. This uniform was phased out during 1954.

The winter field coat was made of wind-resistant cotton/nylon sateen cloth in Olive Green shade 107. It was single-breasted with a five-button front closure, shoulder loops, two lower inside-hanging pockets with flaps, two upper dummy pockets, and sleeves with gusset cuffs and buttons. The coat also had a waist draw-cord threaded through a stitched interior tunnel for adjusting. The same-material hood had button and draw-cord closures and attached to the coat by four buttons. A wool flannel field coat liner was available, and a wool flannel shirt could be worn under the coat.

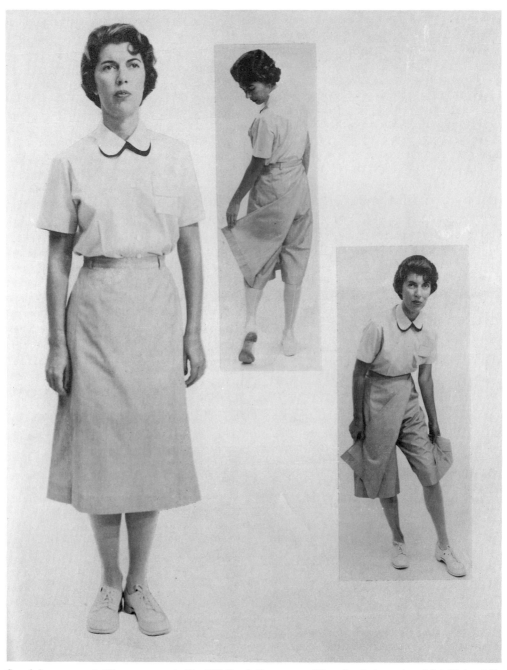

Special-purpose clothing represented by WAC culottes worn with a short-sleeve tan shirt. Note white oxford shoes.

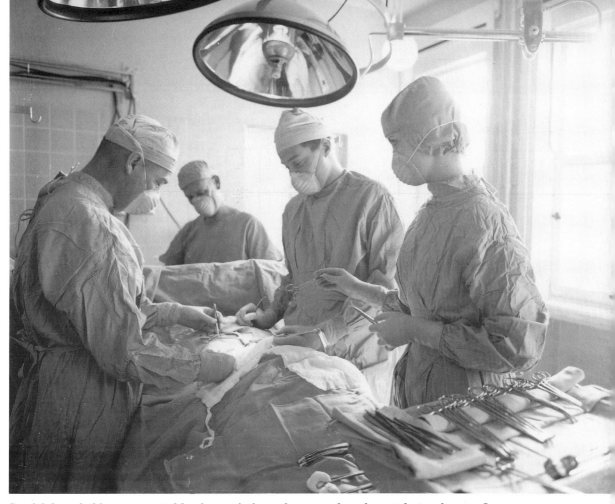

Special-duty clothing represented by the surgical smock, cap, and mask worn by scrub nurse June Richards during an operation at the 2d General Hospital in Landstuhl, Germany, in April 1967.

A new olive green winter field clothing ensemble was authorized on 23 August 1965. The outfit's forest green Olive Green shade 108 gave it the informal "forestry service" nickname. The clothing consisted of olive green wool serge garrison cap and field coat, tan cotton shirt (with black neck tab), and olive green wool serge field skirt or slacks. The mountain-cabin look was highlighted by the alternative field outfit, an Olive Green shade 108 wool flannel shirt worn in coat fashion with the olive green wool serge field slacks.[21]

The wool serge Olive Green shade 108 field coat was a fully lined hip-length, loose-fitting garment with a box-bottom styling. It was single-breasted with a five-button front closure, convertible collar, and shoulder loops, and it had two upper patch pockets and two lower patch pockets with concealed-button flaps.

The wool serge field skirt in Olive Green shade 108 was designed in six-gore style. It had a two-button placket opening on each side, and both front and back waistbands with three-button adjusting tabs. The field slacks were made of the same material as the skirt, and had pockets on each side with two-button closures, and waistbands of the same pattern used on the field skirt.

Other winter field uniform items included the Olive Green shade 107 cold-weather cap, the acrylic double-piqué knitted cardigan-type sweater in Green shade 279, and black leather gloves. Footwear consisted of black low-quarter oxfords, black high-quarter service shoes, or black leather service boots. The black beret was authorized for issuance starting in 1975.

223

1. "Research and Development," *Quartermaster Review,* March–April 1956, p. 54. See the author's *U.S. Army Uniforms of the Korean War* in this uniforms series.
2. SR 600-37-2, Change 6, 13 May 1954, and AR 670-30, Para. 22-27, 25 August 1966.
3. AR 670-30, Change 2, 2 February 1961.
4. DA Circular 670-36, 10 March 1959.
5. DA Circular 670-30, 29 September 1958. Also see the author's *U.S. Army Uniforms of the Vietnam War,* pp. 85–90, in this uniforms series.
6. AR 670-30, Change 3, 22 July 1961.
7. TM 10-229, Para. 19, and Table 1, 20 June 1969.
8. TM 10-229, Para. 20, 20 June 1969.
9. AR 700-8400-1, Change 15, 20 May 1966.
10. *Army Personnel Newsletter No. 2-60,* February 1960, p. 4.
11. AR 670-33, 3 April 1962; AR 670-33, 23 July 1962; and AR 700-8400-1, Change 10, 9 August 1963.
12. DA Circular 670-3, 12 May 1960. The green raincoat is described in the author's *U.S. Army Uniforms of the Vietnam War,* p. 86.
13. SR 600-37-2, Change 7, 13 June 1957.
14. AR 670-30, Para. 4-4, 12 May 1969.
15. AR 670-30, Change 4, 5 July 1962.
16. DA Circular 670-41, 4 September 1959.
17. AR 670-30, 20 October 1959.
18. SR 600-37-10, 16 September 1952.
19. AR 670-30, 20 October 1959.
20. CTA 50-901, 5 October 1966.
21. CTA 50-901, Change 3, 23 August 1965.

12

Cold- and Wet-Weather Clothing

Field Coats

The Army field jacket or coat was designed as a wind-resistant cloth shell for upper body protection, and it could be reinforced with a liner. On 27 March 1953 the Army officially redesignated the M1951 field jacket shell as the M1951 field coat, but soldiers continued to use the more familiar term "field jacket" instead of the official terminology of field coat.

Earlier Olive Drab shade 7 field jackets were considered incompatible with the olive green field coloration scheme. They were comparable to the M1951 field coat in design, however, and thus retained in clothing inventories for distribution on a substitute basis. These included the M1943 field jacket (fitted with interior buttons to accept the liner), the 1949-pattern MQ1 field jacket, and the M1950 field jacket.[1]

The M1951 field coat, as a uniform item, benefitted from its ability to withstand rugged wear under adverse field conditions and still present a suitable military appearance for garrison duties. On 16 November 1956 the field coat was redesignated in accordance with its coloration as the M1951 olive green wind-resistant cotton sateen field coat.

It was made primarily of 9-ounce wind-resistant, water-repellent treated cotton sateen cloth in Olive Green shade 107, and was fully lined with similarly treated 5.5-ounce cotton oxford. The coat contained four large pockets with snap-fastened flaps (two upper patch-type and two lower inside-hanging type), a plain collar, shoulder loops, a slide-fastened front closure, and an elastic draw cord at the hem. The waist draw cord allowed some flexibility in fitting, and the button-attached hood and liner could be added when needed.[2]

The M1951 field coat liner furnished an extra layer of material that trapped warm air between the garments and further shielded the soldier against the cold. The liner was made of moth-repellent, natural 15- to 18.5-ounce double-faced mohair-wool frieze and was edged in Olive Green shade 106 nylon oxford cloth. The liner was adequate for insulating purposes in temperate climates.[3]

During 1960 the Army began designing an improved coat as part of a new experimental inte-

Drill Sergeant Staff Sgt. William Waldron wears the M1951 field coat with service hat as he leads new recruits in army green uniforms during basic training with the 9th Inf Div at Fort Riley, Kansas, in April 1966. He wears individual equipment belt, whistle, and Drill Sergeant identification badge on coat.

Seventh Army commander Lt. Gen. Hugh Harris (*left*) has block cap and field coat, and 2d Armd Div CG Edwin Burba has field coat with elastic cord adjusted at waist, at Spesbach, Germany, during October 1963. Note the fur-pile trimmed visor of the field cap preferred by Seventh Army in Europe, and commercial Dehner tanker boots of General Burba.

Enlisted personnel of the 7774th Signal Bn wear M1943 field jackets beside a K-44 repair truck in Heidelberg, Germany, during 1949. Note the double-breasted mackinaws, issued to drivers and support personnel, worn by two standing figures (*second and third from right*).

grated field clothing system. The system was developed to give the soldier one flexible set of clothing and gear, which could be reconfigured for various combat conditions. Emphasis was placed on protection against hazards such as flame, flash, and chemical-biological-radiological (CBR) agents on the modern battlefield.

A modified field coat, known as the T61-3 cold-weather coat, was announced as part of this system in February 1962. The Olive Green shade 107 cold-weather coat was treated with water-repellent Quarpel, and fold-out cuff extensions were added for better thermal protection of the hands. It had a pullman gas flap fly-closure with slide, Velcro tab fasteners, an improved throat latch, and waist and hem draw cords. In a CBR or thermal environment it was chemically treated in

The M1951 field coats worn by Generals Moore (*left*) and Smith (*right*) contrast with the M1965 pattern worn by officer in background, at Camp Kaiser, Korea, in November 1970. Note the elastic tie-cord fastened on the outside by General Moore.

Sgt. James Brown of the 42d Field Artillery Bn at Grafenwoehr, Germany, during May 1955 has the M1951 field coat, burlap strips worn as camouflage on M1 steel helmet, and M4 bayonet in M8 scabbard for the carbine issued to personnel of field artillery units. Note olive drab and blue NCO insignia of grade on sleeve.

Collar detail of the M-65 cold-weather field coat on Staff Sgt. Raymond Hermann at Fort Bragg, North Carolina, during January 1969. He has camouflage scarf, has subdued pin-on insignia of grade on the collars of his utility shirt, and has retained embroidered insignia of grade on the coat.

Dog handler of the 33d Inf Scout Dog Platoon, 7th Army, gives the command to stay at Grafenwoehr, Germany, in March 1952. He wears the field jacket with fully tightened draw cord, M1949 wool glove inserts, and pile field cap.

the field, the chemical warfare (CW) liner was attached, and the soldier fastened all coat closures, turned up the collar, and tightened the draw cords.[4]

The lightweight T61-3 insulating liner had a collar and buttoned into the cold-weather coat. It could be worn over the CW liner in a CBR environment. The insulating liner was made of Olive Green shade 106 rip-stop nylon cloth, quilted to polyester batting, and a binding of nylon-cotton oxford cloth in Olive Green shade 107. The soldier, however, had to avoid contact with flames or hot stoves because the heat would melt the fabric and cause serious injury.[5]

Further engineer design testing resulted in a more extensive coat modification, known as the T62-4 cold-wet coat, or "ET model" (engineer test model), introduced during February 1963. The experimental cold-wet coat was made of a new

Quarpel-treated nylon cotton sateen cloth. A pull-out, windproof hood was added to the collar, which was redesigned and fitted with a horizontal slide fastener for hood insertion. The hood had a draw cord for tightening over an insulating field cap. Features introduced with the T61-3 cold-weather coat were also retained.[6]

The next experimental coat, known as the T63-5 field coat, was announced as part of the M-65 integrated field-combat clothing system in October 1963 and tested throughout 1964. The test field coat was designed in conformity with the hooded cold-wet coat, but several refinements were incorporated. This design was adopted by the Army on 29 September 1966, and officially designated the M-65 cold-weather field coat on 17 March 1970.

The M-65 cold-weather field coat was a

Maintenance specialists of the 26th Transportation Company repair helicopter engine at Verdun, France, in November 1960. They wear blocked caps with flight jackets, issued to aviation personnel as organizational clothing, and cotton sateen trousers.

sturdy combat garment that offered better warmth and moisture repellency and contained many convenient features for more practical field use. The coat front closure had a combination of a slide-fastener, a snap fastener, and Velcro tabs. The sleeves contained Velcro-adjustable cuffs with hand-shield extensions. The integral lightweight hood could be secured under the collar by a slide-fastened closure. The quilted nylon liner had a collar, open underarms, and buttonhole tabs for attachment to the coat.

Some officers and NCOs objected to the coat's "diminished garrison appeal," because its rounded collar lacked trim styling, the zippered-in

hood had a padded effect that kept the collar in an upright position, and the Velcro closures encouraged untidiness. Nonetheless, the field worthiness of the coat guaranteed troop approval. Further design improvements were incorporated into the cold-weather field coat on 17 August 1973, and the camouflage version was adopted on 3 June 1980.[7]

The "U.S. ARMY" distinguishing insignia had been placed above the upper left pocket of the coat since 27 October 1953. At that time, unit clothing and equipage repair shops were ordered to affix the insignia before issuing the coat. Manufacturers were directed to place the insignia during production "as soon as stocks of this insignia are available," but DA conceded "it is expected that it will be from 1 to 2 years before shipments from depots will have this insignia attached."[8]

The "U.S. ARMY" woven label had golden yellow block lettering on a black background. The name tape could be worn above the right shirt pocket. The label contained the last name in black block lettering on white engineer tape. Starting on 14 July 1966 black lettering was placed on Olive Green shade 107 background for both tapes.[9]

In addition to the standard field coat, commercial winter jackets were also available. One veteran who served in the 62d Tank Battalion at Kitzingen, Germany, during 1956–58, stated:

"The first thing all tankers did upon arriving in Germany was to purchase a tanker's [winter] jacket. This was a zippered jacket that came to the belt line, with knit cuffs, collar, and waist. The outer fabric was a lightweight canvas type of material, and the jacket was well insulated and worn in everything but the coldest weather. It came with a multitude of zippered pockets and loops to hold pens and pencils,

Members of the 195th Avn Company, 5th Army, at Fort Carson, Colorado, at pistol practice in May 1969 wear helmets with the L-2B summer weight reversible flying jacket, which was sage gray-green with an inside orange color labeled international red.

Sgt. First Class David Pressley of the 158th Avn Bn at Fort Riley, Kansas, in November 1968, has embroidered insignia of grade on front of flying jacket because its sleeve pencil pocket prevented normal enlisted rank placement. This practice was outmoded by pin-on collar insignia of grade on his shirt collars.

Capt. Gordon Wood (*right*), 87th Transportation Detachment commander, wears an intermediate flying jacket with fur collar instead of the coat to his army green uniform at Verdun, France, in November 1960. The Army unit was attached to an Air Force command.

etc. I even saw officers with leather patches on theirs. These jackets for tank crewmen wouldn't get caught on the various pieces of equipment in the tank. This was a good idea but everybody in armor units wore them—clerks, cooks, medics, everybody. The reason was they looked sharp. They were purchased from German tailors who also sold civilian clothing to the troops."[10]

Overcoats

At the conclusion of World War II the old roll-collar wool melton enlisted overcoat was still in Army inventory, despite its antiquated military appearance and unsatisfactory wearing qualities. Known as the "horse blanket," it continued to be worn with the garrison uniform until replaced by the Olive Drab shade 7 field overcoat with removable liner. This transition was largely completed during the winter of 1953–54, when all wool melton enlisted overcoats were withdrawn from active clothing stocks in most overseas depots and stateside stations.

The olive drab field overcoat was produced under specifications approved on 7 June 1946, and was immediately favored by the troops because of its military appearance and weather-protective qualities. The field overcoat was worn with the winter uniform and as the standard overcoat for military formations. A commercial-pattern olive drab wool muffler was permitted on an optional basis.

The overcoat was made of 5-ounce wind-resistant and water-repellent cotton twill or poplin, and its buttoned-in removable liner was made of olive drab wool material. The double-breasted overcoat contained shoulder loops, a convertible-style roll collar, and notched lapels. It also had two front slash welt pockets, a belt, and sleeve tabs.[11]

An improved M1950 Olive Drab shade 7 field overcoat with removable liner was produced under specifications dated 15 February 1951. This final olive drab overcoat version contained cotton poplin "leggings," or extensions designed to secure the overcoat to a soldier's legs while marching.[12]

The Olive Green shade 107 cotton sateen overcoat with removable liner, also known as the

The officers' Taupe shade 79 wool gabardine overcoat (*left*) contrasts with the Army Green shade 44 wool gabardine overcoat, which replaced it, at the Army Armor Center, Fort Knox, Kentucky, during 1967.

"field overcoat," was produced under specifications dated 12 November 1952. Designed like the olive drab field overcoat, it was made of wind-resistant, water-repellent cotton sateen cloth and lined with cotton oxford cloth. The overcoat was phased into the Army supply system from 1953

235

Officers at Fort Leonard Wood, Missouri, wear Taupe shade 79 wool gabardine overcoats, known as "trench coats," during January 1962. Brig. Gen. James Cash wears an intermediate flying jacket with fur collar (*second from right*).

through 1955. First priority was given to the Far East Command and Alaska, and the process was extended to forces in Europe and other overseas commands beginning in August 1953. The overcoat was distributed in the continental United States throughout the following year.

The overcoat harmonized with the Army's olive green color scheme for field clothing, and the olive drab overcoat was phased out in stages. Effective 1 September 1953 officers and warrant officers were not allowed to wear the olive drab overcoat except in the field. On 4 February 1955 the olive green overcoat became the enlisted garrison overcoat, by which time the Taupe shade 179 overcoat was the only one used by officers.[13]

One officer described the transition from field overcoats:

"The field overcoats were disappearing when I came on active duty [in 1953] and my first uniform purchases included one of the then relatively new taupe trench coats. Unfortunately the division commander of my first unit, the 47th Infantry Division, decided he had to improve the appearance (or maybe the conformity) of the officers. He decreed that at the next Saturday inspection, then an institution, all officers would be standing in front of their troops with their field coat folded over their left forearm so that he could check as he walked by or drove by the formations. This caused a panic among lieutenants as very few owned them, nobody wanted to have them because they were not permitted for wear other than in the field where the field jacket was adequate, and everybody

First Army commander Maj. Gen. Thomas Herren (*left*) and Brig. Gen. Einar Gjelsteen wear Taupe shade 79 wool gabardine trench coats with olive drab service caps and Olive Drab shade 33 wool serge trousers at Fort Devens, Massachusetts, in August 1954.

Artillery commanders at Darmstadt, Germany, wear Taupe shade 79 overcoats and Olive Drab shade 54 trousers in November 1955. Note the head straps of their fur felt service caps, wool mufflers, gloves, and swagger sticks.

Musicians of the 9th Army Band in Alaska during 1963 wear Olive Green shade 107 field overcoats, nylon twill Taupe shade 179 raincoat, and the officers' Taupe shade 79 overcoat (*second from right*), which was optional for enlisted men but not issued to them. Note wear of insignia on overcoats.

knew that they were soon to go out of inventory. It looked like a choice between an Article 15 [punishment] or a useless purchase from our meager pay until one of my clever peers discovered that the sleeping bag cover could be folded and pressed into a very passable semblance of a folded officers' field coat. The word spread quickly and the pompous general must have looked at the folds of about 400 sleeping bag covers without ever detecting the scam. I must admit that there was considerable nervousness that he might direct everyone to put their coats on so that he could check the fit. Fortunately for a lot of careers, this did not happen."[14]

Officers were authorized the Taupe shade 79 overcoat, known as the "trench coat," which was phased into use on an optional basis on 22 June 1949. On 1 September 1953 it became the required overcoat for officers in garrison, and became the sole officer overcoat after 18 February 1953, when officers were prohibited from wearing the olive green overcoat with field clothing. The taupe overcoat was optional for enlisted men.[15]

The trench coat design and color gave the taupe overcoat a dignified appearance that was widely regarded within the officer corps as traditional officer-grade styling. The overcoat was made of 14.5- to 16-ounce wool gabardine and had a buttoned-in, removable wool lining. The overcoat was double-breasted with a convertible collar and notched lapels, shoulder loops, a rain-protective yoke for the right shoulder, sleeve tabs, and two lower slash welt pockets. The self-material belt, with taupe plastic buckle, was supported with belt loops. The removable olive drab wool liner was attached with buttons in earlier models, and later with a slide fastener.[16]

The olive drab wool muffler continued to be authorized for overcoats. On 5 November 1957 an Army Green shade 44 woven wool scarf, or an alternate silk or woven rayon scarf in Army Green shade 279, was authorized with the taupe overcoat when worn over the army green uniform. At this time, the wool muffler was restricted to either enlisted soldiers wearing the olive green overcoat or to officers wearing the "pinks and greens" olive drab wool uniform.[17]

The Army Green shade 44 wool gabardine overcoat was developed to replace both the olive green overcoat (worn by enlisted personnel) and the taupe overcoat (worn by officers and warrant officers). On 18 August 1964 specifications for the overcoat were adopted, and it was issued to inductees starting on 24 August 1967. The taupe and olive green overcoats became obsolete 1 July 1970.[18]

The army green overcoat, also known as the "trench coat," was made of 14.5-ounce wool gabardine, had a removable liner, and was designed identically to the taupe overcoat. Despite this design similarity, the green coloration was perceived by many officers as lacking the authority of the classic taupe shade. The army green overcoat, however, harmonized with the army green uniform and was worn by all ranks. The overcoat could be worn with an Army Green shade 44 wool (or silk or rayon) scarf.

Wet-Weather Clothing

The Army postwar inventory contained a variety of raincoats. Unfortunately, most were produced in World War II and their fabric coatings were curtailed by wartime rubber shortages, a factor that made them unsuitable for sustained wear. An improved dismounted olive drab synthetic rubber coated raincoat was adopted in 1949 and produced according to specifications approved on 7 July 1950. This was the standard raincoat for enlisted personnel and was used for field and garrison duty until replaced by the army green shade over a decade later.[19]

Officers and warrant officers could wear the outer shell of their olive drab or taupe overcoats as raincoats, or acquire civilian non-transparent raincoats with shoulder loops in olive drab or, after

The Quarpel-treated Army Green shade 274 raincoat is worn by USMA Superintendent Maj. Gen. Donald Bennet as he extends condolences to the wife of an aviation officer killed in Vietnam, during the burial service at West Point, New York, in October 1967.

Field rain gear worn by members of the 197th Inf Bde while at Fort Stewart, Georgia, during 1964. The captain wears a Taupe shade 179 raincoat (*left*) while coordinating with a sergeant in lightweight olive green poncho with hood.

1955, olive green or taupe. An officer recalled the situation:

"A penultimate uniform memory was the officer's raincoat. There was not one authorized. For some reason it was forbidden to use the field raincoat issued to enlisted men, even when in the field. Not that anyone really wanted to. In all save sub-zero weather they soon became sweat boxes and you would be wetter from sweat than any rain could do. Additionally, it was clearly a field item, not meant for garrison wear over the ODs, "pinks and greens," or the new green uniforms then starting to be seen. So every officer had a different raincoat. Five officers standing together would have five different raincoats. One officer in my battalion wore a cadet raincoat that he had dyed. I had one of an oily cloth made by some outfit called Alligator which met the Army's only criteria: it was olive drab. It, unlike many, shed rain."[20]

The Taupe shade 179 raincoat was adopted by QMCTC 3-57 and was used by all ranks. Officers were required to own it after 1 April 1959.

Rubberized nylon wet-weather parkas are worn with high five-buckle overshoes by troops of the 1st Cavalry Division in Korea during 1963. Waterproof parkas were favored by line soldiers and other personnel, such as firing range instructors, and worn over the field utility uniforms.

The double-breasted raincoat, made of 1.6-ounce nylon twill, had a lapel collar, shoulder loops, sleeve tabs, inside hanging pockets, and a self-belt with plastic slide buckle. The raincoat interior was waterproofed with a polyvinyl butyryl coating. Unfortunately, the taupe raincoat discolored when wet and clung to the wearer's lower body during movement, and its fabric impermeability caused moisture condensation to accumulate on the inside of the garment.[21]

A veteran remarked, "When the army specified a raincoat, it was flat awful. It was taupe color and very thin nylon-like material. It leaked about the seams. It was so light that the skirt of it blew up to the waist in any breeze (I put curtain weights in the skirt of mine). And the 3-inch-wide belt was so lacking in any stiffness that it quickly became a quarter-inch rope around the waist."[22]

These problems, which plagued all fabric-coated raincoats to some degree, were not resolved until the Army developed a new water-repellent treatment labeled Quarpel. After extensive testing, the Army adopted the Quarpel-treated army green raincoat in Army Green shade 274 on 18 August 1964. In addition to offering improved washability and wearing qualities, it harmonized with the army

242

green uniform and complemented its year-round basis of wear as the standard service uniform. By 1 July 1968 the taupe nylon raincoat was replaced within the supply system by the army green raincoat, and the former raincoat was declared obsolete on 1 July 1971.[23]

The army green raincoat was worn by all ranks with service and dress uniforms. It was made of a single layer of 5-ounce cotton/nylon oxford cloth, treated with water-repellent Quarpel. The raincoat was issued to inductees starting on 1 July 1966 and became mandatory for wear on 1 July 1970.

Other wet-weather gear included the poncho,

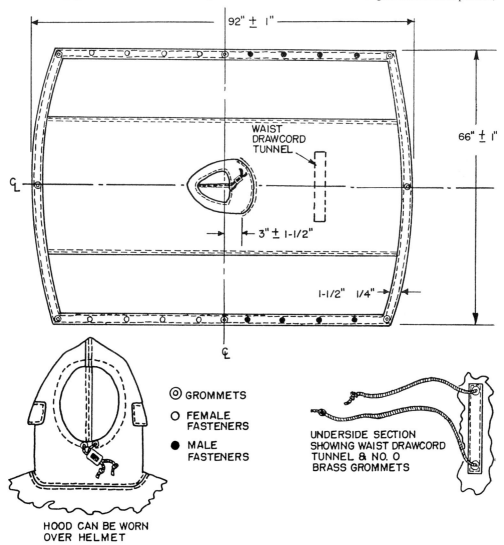

Olive Green shade 207 nylon-coated poncho with hood.

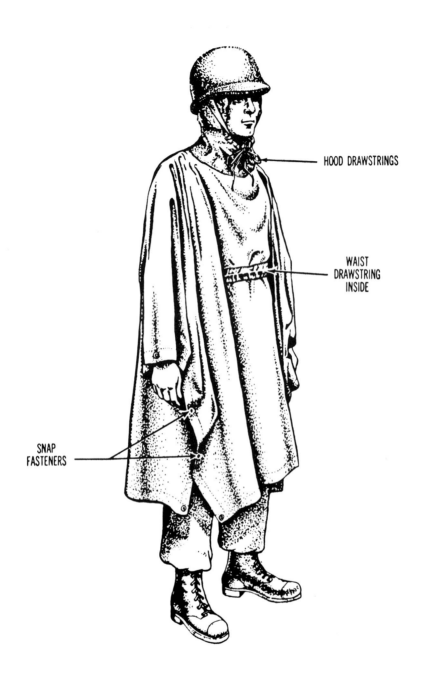

HOOD DRAWSTRINGS

WAIST
DRAWSTRING
INSIDE

SNAP
FASTENERS

Soldier wearing poncho as rain garment.

which was the soldier's field mainstay against inclement weather. The poncho as a rain cape gave better protection than a raincoat in the field, because its size and hooded design enabled the soldier to be covered comfortably while carrying equipment. The poncho also fulfilled a variety of other purposes, such as providing a ground cover underneath the sleeping bag, serving as an extra covering for warmth, or combining with another poncho to form an expedient tent-shelter.

The World War II–era olive drab lightweight poncho, revised on 23 September 1949, was made of nylon twill and was coated with vinyl resin on both sides. The head opening had a raised collar that closed with a drawstring. In 1950 a hood was added, and this pattern was produced as the olive drab lightweight poncho with hood under specifications dated 18 September 1951.

The same poncho design was adopted in olive green field coloration on 2 November 1953 and redesignated as the Olive Green shade 207 nylon coated poncho with hood. It had curved ends, and measured 66 inches wide and 92 inches long along center lines. The poncho was seamed lengthwise and made from a center panel (preferably the full width of the fabric), with two strips joined so that the fold of the seam faced the outside edge. The neck opening was positioned forward of the center, and the attached hood was fitted with a draw cord and slide keeper. The sides of the poncho were fitted with grommets and double-snap fasteners that were used to form sleeves when the poncho was used in the role of a rain cape, or to join ponchos together when making combination shelters.[24]

The olive green nylon coated poncho remained standard until superseded by improved lightweight and camouflage ponchos in response to the combat requirements of the Vietnam conflict. The development of these later ponchos and poncho liners are detailed in the author's *U.S. Army Uniforms of the Vietnam War.*

Cold-Weather Field Clothing

Army winter field clothing was designed to meet the demands of either cold-wet or cold-dry weather conditions. A cold-wet environment subjected soldiers to near-freezing temperatures, often accompanied by rain or wet snow and muddy or sloshy terrain. Army clothing developed for these circumstances consisted of water-repellent, wind-resistant outer layers worn over an insulated inner layer. Cold-dry weather conditions exposed soldiers to colder temperatures below 14 degrees Fahrenheit, strong winds, dry powdery snow, and frozen ground. A different system of clothing was devised to provide complete body protection against the wind, along with additional insulating layers to shield against the severe cold.[25]

The Army cold-wet and the cold-dry uniform systems were thus composed of inner, intermediate, and outer layers with specialized headgear, gloves and mittens, and footwear. The systems insulated the soldier against heat loss by combining up to six layers (including liners) that trapped warm air between clothing, and used tightly woven Quarpel-treated outer fabric for wind and water resistance. The clothing layers could be adjusted to meet changing environmental conditions through removable layers and adjustable openings, closures, and drawstrings.

The first (inner) layer consisted of cushion sole socks and 50-50 cotton/wool underwear with a loose-fitting design for unimpeded circulation and ventilation. The drawers and additional layers of trousers were supported by the scissors-type suspenders worn over the undershirt.

The second layer in the cold-wet uniform system consisted of the Olive Green shade 108 wool/nylon field shirt and trousers. The second layer of the cold-dry uniform system combined the same field shirt with Olive Green shade 107 wind-resistant sateen M1951 field trouser shells and M1951 field trouser liners, made of mohair frieze and later quilted nylon.

The outer layer of the cold-wet uniform system consisted of the M1951 field coat and M1951 arctic trouser shells, along with black rubber insulated boots, insulating helmet-liner cap, coat liner and hood, and wool and leather gloves. The same layer existed for the cold-dry uniform system but served as an intermediate layer, except for footwear consisting of white rubber insulated boots.

M1951 arctic trouser shells, developed during the Korean War and produced under specifications approved on 21 February 1952, were procured in sufficient quantity only after hostilities ended. The arctic trouser shells were made of nylon/cotton oxford cloth in Olive Green shade

The outer layer of the cold-dry uniform system is worn at Camp Century, Greenland, during May 1964. It consisted of M1951 pile field caps and parkas, arctic trouser liners, and winter combat boots. Gen. Noel Parrish (*center*) wears garrison cap, AF parka, and mukluk boots.

107, and had leg, hem, and waistband draw cords, suspender loops, and a slide-fastened fly. The trousers had one patch pocket on the hip, two side band openings with snap-closed flaps, and two side cargo pockets with tiecords.[26]

The fourth or outer layer of the cold-dry uniform system consisted of the M1951 parka and its removable mohair/frieze liner. The three-quarter-length parka had a combination slide and snap-

fastened front fly closure, adjustable cuffs, waist and hem draw cords, and a split lower back. The liner was made of quilted nylon. The system also included arctic trouser liners, fur-ruff hood, over-whites, and appropriate mittens and gloves.

The Quartermaster Research and Engineering Command developed a helmet liner insulator that was field-tested by the Army Arctic Test Board during the winter of 1961–62, and adopted

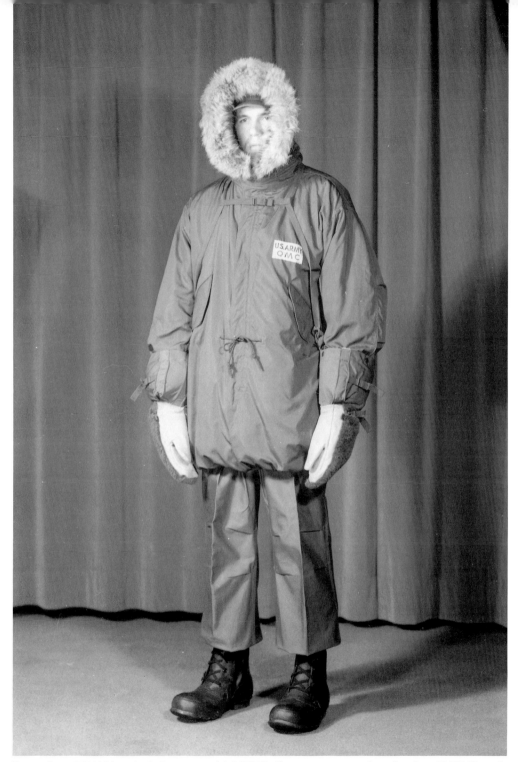

Front view of M1951 parka being worn with M1951 olive green cotton winter hood and M1949 arctic mitten set strapped over coat. Note black rubber cold-wet insulated boots.

Rear view of M1951 parka with detachable fur-trimmed hoods, showing the split lower backside of the parka. Soldiers are carrying their field packs by the strap handles during this troop movement.

by DA in 1964 as the M-65 insulating helmet liner to replace the M1951 field pile cap. The Quarpel-treated nylon/cotton oxford head cover had no visor and was designed to be worn under the helmet or hood. It had a close-fitting crown with a napped acrilan lining, a combination earflap-neck protector with back stretch panel lined with nylon knit fleece, and alpaca-lined forehead flap with Velcro tab ends. When worn by itself, the lower flap could be folded around the top with the Velcro fastening tabs crisscrossed in front.[27]

The M1951 olive green cotton winter hood was worn fastened to the integral hood of the M1951 parka. Several improvements were made in this "fur-ruff hood" following the Korean War. A malleable wire inside the fur ruff could be shaped as desired for greater face protection. The fur ruff was manufactured of either alum-tanned fur or chrome-tanned fur, but only the latter would withstand laundering. On 31 July 1963 DA changed the hood specification to mandate use of chrome-tanned fur in its production. The M-65 winter fur-ruff hood was larger and contained Velcro front fasteners and a two-piece shaped storm curtain.[28]

Nose and cheek protection was gained by covering as much of the face as possible with the wool scarf. It was adjusted from time to time, and rotated whenever the portion next to the mouth and nose became covered with frost. The frozen end was left outside the coat or parka. The cold-weather mask was used during high winds, but it had to be removed periodically to check for frostbite.

During 1971 Natick Laboratories began engineer testing on a lightweight cold-weather mask that offered facial protection in severe cold, at minus 65 degrees Fahrenheit with 35 mile-per-hour wind velocity. The facepiece was made of laminated insulating material and weighed about 2½ ounces. It had a wide vision port between the forehead and lower face portions, and a removable front thermal barrier (designed like a pollen mask), affixed by Velcro tabs over the mouth and nose.

Standard M1949 black leather glove shells were worn with M1949 wool glove inserts. Lightweight cotton work gloves with leather palms gave better finger dexterity, but only provided protection against the cold for short periods. M1951 trigger-finger mitten shells were worn with M1948 wool trigger-finger inserts during moderately cold weather.

The T63-5 integrated field combat clothing system was adopted during 1964 as the M-65 components. This view shows the cold-dry uniform system with overwhites and white rubber insulated boots. The garments and liners are opened, showing successive layers of upper-body clothing down to the undershirt.

The M1949 arctic mitten set was used for colder weather. The gauntlet-styled arctic mittens were made of wind-resistant sateen in Olive Green shade 107, a saddle-shade top-grain deerskin leather palm with thumb, wool/alpaca pile and cotton back, and back fasteners. The mitten set was attached to a neck strap for ease of carriage, while snapped together behind the back, which helped prevent mitten loss.

The black rubber cold-wet insulated boots were designed specifically for combat troops who had little opportunity for frequent changes of socks. The boots were made of black latex and calendered rubber compound with a rubber-chevron cleated rigid-type sole, a rubber cleated heel, and full lacing to the top. The insulating material was hermetically sealed into the sides and bottoms of the boots, and this improvement dispensed with

The M1950 overwhite parka with hood, trousers, mittens, and rucksack cover is being worn for snow camouflage by a soldier of the 172d Inf Bde at Fort Richardson, Alaska, in 1970.

The M-65 winter fur-ruff hood is worn over the M-65 insulating helmet liner with Velcro-fastened flaps by soldiers of the 171st Inf Bde southeast of Nome, Alaska, in December 1969. Note Geneva Convention brassard worn by medic Pfc. Earl Court (*center*).

Army chemical protective suiting is represented by the M3 Toxicological Agents Protective (TAP) ensemble, being worn by a hospital hazards material team during training at Fort Devens, Massachusetts, in April 1970.

Dog handlers and dog training instructor wore the heavily padded dog attack training coat and trousers, with the burlap dog attack training cuff, as shown by Sgt. Benny Clay of the 18th MP Bde in 1970.

the need for removable inner soles and a second layer of socks.[29]

These "Mickey Mouse" boots were useful in snow, slush, mud, and cold water. Only one pair of cushion-sole socks was worn to avoid cramping the feet and restricting blood circulation. The boots kept the feet warm while in position or on guard, but they were difficult to march in because they tended to saw against the leg at mid-calf. The boots were inadequate for prolonged wear in temperatures below minus 20 degrees Fahrenheit. Soldiers could make quick-fix boot repairs with ordinary tire patching or air-mattress patching material, friction tape, and even chewing gum.

Engineer fire fighters wear the firemen's plastic helmet and Olive Drab shade 7 firemen's flame-resistant cotton duck coat and trousers while training on the burning fuselage of an old DC-4 aircraft during 1967.

The fire fighters' aluminum asbestos ensemble, as shown at a military installation during 1969. The ensemble was used when more complete protection was required, such as in rescue work, when handling extremely hazardous materials, or during fire-fighting situations involving exploding fuel.

By 1971 exploratory engineer development had commenced on a LINCLOE micro-cellular urethane-coated boot with outsoles and unit-molded upper portions. Each boot weighed only 23 ounces. The pull-on "semi-jackboot" style boots were easy to put on or take off, and the "Vibram" design gave good traction. The close-fitting ankle design provided adequate ankle support.

The white rubber cold-dry insulated boots with release valve were designed to protect the feet in temperatures as low as minus 60 degrees Fahrenheit. The boots were made of white latex and calendered rubber compound with a seamless inner and outer carcass and sealed insulation. They were worn over one pair of cushion-sole socks. The outside air-release valve provided parachutists with a means of equalizing external and internal air pressures when undergoing altitude changes. The valve was closed at all other times to prevent moisture from reaching the boot's insulation and rendering it unserviceable.

The M1950 overwhites were winter camou-

The Fort Leavenworth Army Disciplinary Barracks pistol team members wear the cotton coats authorized for marksmanship teams during 1961. The service hats have cords worn by marksmanship teams.

flage consisting of trousers, mittens, and a lightweight parka with hood. White covers were also issued for the rucksack. The cotton jean fabric was prepared by a special bleaching process, including optical brighteners following a treatment with a fluorocarbon water and soil repellent finish. The complete white suit was worn when the ground was covered completely by snow, and suit portions were mixed with regular outer field clothing when the ground was covered only by snow patches.

Handling stoves, digging in ground, and performing other field tasks soiled the overwhites quickly, and they had to be washed and changed frequently to retain their snow-camouflage properties. Like other winter clothing, the overwhites became frosty and icy after use and the frost had to be removed to expedite drying.

1. Field jacket evolution is detailed in the author's *U.S. Army Uniforms of World War II,* p. 85, and *U.S. Army Uniforms of the Korean War,* pp. 40–49.
2. MIL-J-11448.
3. MIL-L-11449.
4. US Army Quartermaster Research and Engineering Command, *Clothing and Equipment Development Branch Series Report No. 26,* February 1962, p. 57.
5. *Ibid.,* p. 61.
6. US Army Quartermaster Research and Engineering Command, *Clothing and Equipment Development Branch Series Report No. 37,* February 1963, p. 55.
7. MIL-C-43455.
8. DA Circular 106, 27 October 1953.
9. DA Circular 106, 27 October 1953.
10. Bill Berebitsky ltr to author, 7 December 1992.
11. MIL-O-2419.
12. MIL-O-2419A. This overcoat is illustrated in the author's *U.S. Army Uniforms of the Korean War,* p. 61.
13. DA Circular 25, 6 April 1953, and DA Circular 44, 15 June 1953; SR 600-32-1, Change 3, 4 February 1955.
14. Scot Crerar correspondence to author, 26 November 1992.
15. SR 600-32-1, Change 3, 4 February 1955.
16. MIL-O-3219.
17. AR 670-5, Change 12, 5 November 1957.
18. DA Message 982678, 18 August 1964, and AR 670-5, Para. 13-11, 23 September 1966.
19. MIL-R-2259.
20. Scot Crerar correspondence.
21. MIL-R-14508 and DA Circular 670-31, 28 October 1958.
22. Scot Crerar correspondence.
23. DA Message 982678, 18 August 1964.
24. MIL-P-3003.
25. FM 31-70, 24 February 1959.
26. MIL-T-11786.
27. Army Test and Evaluation Command, *Final Report of Confirmatory Test (Type II) of Helmet Liner Insulator,* 21 May 1964, and related documents.
28. Army Test and Evaluation Command, *Final Test Report for the Integrated Combat Uniform,* 12 June 1964, p. 4.
29. MIL-B-15094.

APPENDIX I

Barracks Clothing and Equipment Displays

Army soldiers were required to maintain and display their clothing and individual equipment in accordance with strictly enforced prescribed standards. This procedure enabled ready inspection to ensure serviceability, appearance, and accountability—soldiers having personally signed for most of their individual equipment. Shortcomings in either of these areas potentially compromised the unit mission and adversely affected personal health, comfort, and safety.

The Army passion for high standards of maintenance reached almost a fetish, especially between the Korean and Vietnam wars. Under the eyes of seasoned Regular Army NCOs, peacetime draftees learned to make their bunks, polish their brass insignia, and spit-shine their shoes and boots. Soldiers arranged their issue items in a prearranged form dictated by the unit's standard operating procedure (SOP) to pass their officers' inspection. This level of control over the environment of soldiers billeted in government barracks was most exacting in basic combat or advanced individual training, and was reemphasized during attendance at officer candidate schools or NCO academies.

The postwar soldier lived in an open squad bay of a barracks with approximately sixty or more enlisted personnel. Most soldiers were quartered, at least while undergoing training, in the linear-style barracks of the World War II wooden-frame temporary mobilization buildings. Larger squad bays were available in spacious 1930s-era buildings, typified by western Spanish-style stucco or eastern Georgian red brick structures, as well as in the 1950s-style concrete-block masonry units. Soldiers stationed overseas often lived in square-room barracks, such as those found in the German *kaserne* establishments.

The soldier slept on a thin mattress placed on the simple springs of a tubular steel folding cot. Each man slept between two white sheets and had a small pillow and two wool blankets from company supply. The cots were arranged in rows, head to foot, down each side of the bay, and could be stacked using metal bunk adapters.

All issue items had a precise location in the soldier's area. Outer clothing was fully buttoned and arranged on wire hangers on a shelf or inside a metal wall locker, with headgear placed uppermost. The footlocker, kept at the end of the bunk, contained neatly rolled underwear and towels underneath a removable upper tray, in which rolled socks and toilet articles were placed. Every draftee remembers purchasing from the PX his inspection

SOP kit of matching toiletries—used only for display. Footwear was arranged in order underneath the bunk, often marked with red or white dots to indicate daily rotation. Individual equipment was assembled and suspended from the bunk ends. Cardboard was placed inside the field pack to create the square shape desired for inspection.

The squad bay was inspected daily, and a formal inspection occurred once a week to determine whether all clothing and equipment was present, serviceable, and properly marked. The latter inspections were usually held on Saturday mornings during training, and were known as "stand-by" inspections because the soldier stood beside his bunk and equipment.

The different kinds of inspections determined how individual clothing and equipment items were displayed. During "showdown" command inspections the soldier presented a full equipment display, known as "junk on the bunk," wherein the contents of his field pack and other equipment were laid out on the cot. This manner of arrangement was derived from the traditional "full field" equipment display during inspection in ranks, wherein each soldier would ground his weapon and open the pack in front of his pitched shelter tent.

Every garment was required to be marked with the soldier's individual number (composed of the first letter of the last name and the last four digits of the army service number) since 1942. By 1964 identification was only required on headgear, footgear, waist belt, and duffel bag, and these items were marked using the full name and service number.

SHELF DISPLAY

LEFT TO RIGHT : ON SHELF
  HELMET   HELMET LINER
  CAP, SERVICE   CAP, GARRISON

LEFT TO RIGHT : ON HANGERS
  CIVILIAN CLOTHES
  SHIRT, COTTON OVER TROUSERS
  SHIRT, POPLIN
  JACKET, WOOL, O.D. OVER TROUSERS
  FATIGUE JACKET OVER FATIGUE TROUSERS
  COAT, COTTON
  OVERCOAT
  WASHCLOTH OVER TOWEL

WALL LOCKER DISPLAY

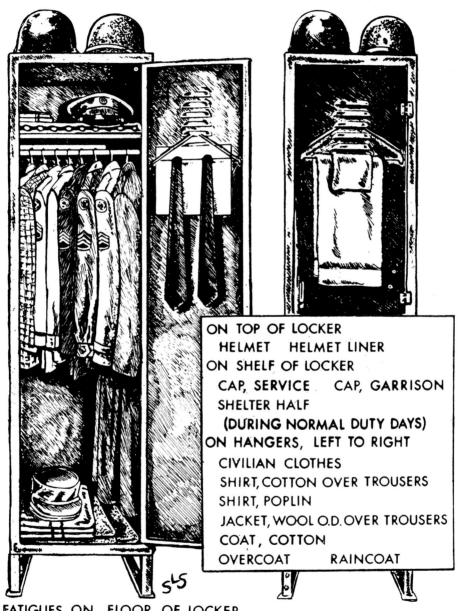

ON TOP OF LOCKER
  HELMET   HELMET LINER
ON SHELF OF LOCKER
  CAP, SERVICE   CAP, GARRISON
  SHELTER HALF
  (DURING NORMAL DUTY DAYS)
ON HANGERS, LEFT TO RIGHT
  CIVILIAN CLOTHES
  SHIRT, COTTON OVER TROUSERS
  SHIRT, POPLIN
  JACKET, WOOL O.D. OVER TROUSERS
  COAT, COTTON
  OVERCOAT   RAINCOAT

FATIGUES ON FLOOR OF LOCKER

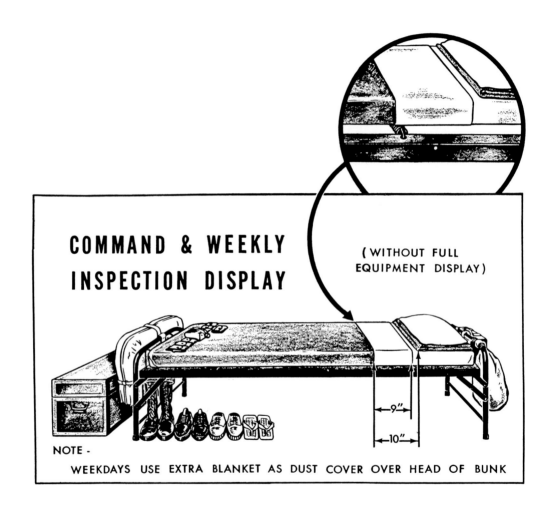

COMMAND & WEEKLY
INSPECTION DISPLAY

(WITHOUT FULL
EQUIPMENT DISPLAY)

9"

10"

NOTE -

WEEKDAYS USE EXTRA BLANKET AS DUST COVER OVER HEAD OF BUNK

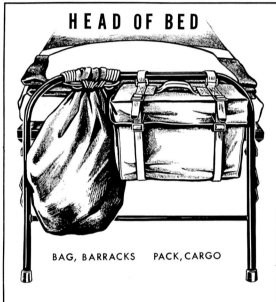

HEAD OF BED

BAG, BARRACKS   PACK, CARGO

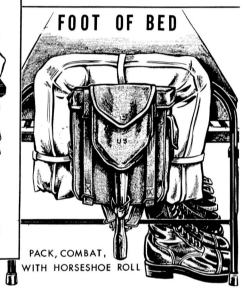

FOOT OF BED

PACK, COMBAT,
WITH HORSESHOE ROLL

(HORSESHOE ROLL FOR INSPECTIONS ONLY)

FOOT LOCKER DISPLAY

TRAY –   TOILET ARTICLES   HANDKERCHIEFS
SHOE POLISH   SHOE BRUSH   SOCKS

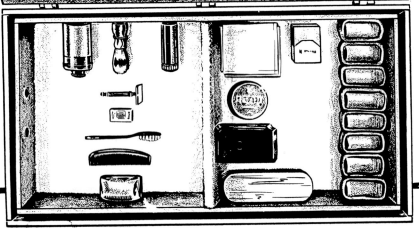

BOTTOM – GLOVES   SOCKS   BELTS   TOILET KIT
UNDERCLOTHING,   LEFT TO RIGHT :
UNDERSHIRTS, WOOLEN   DRAWERS, WOOLEN
UNDERSHIRTS, COTTON   DRAWERS, COTTON
TOWELS

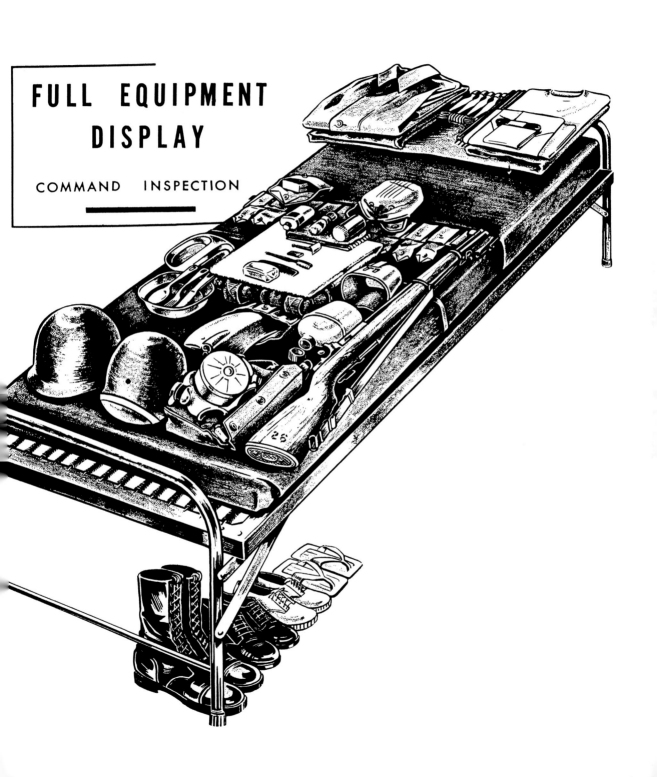

FULL EQUIPMENT
DISPLAY

COMMAND INSPECTION

FULL FIELD
EQUIPMENT DISPLAY

IN THE FIELD

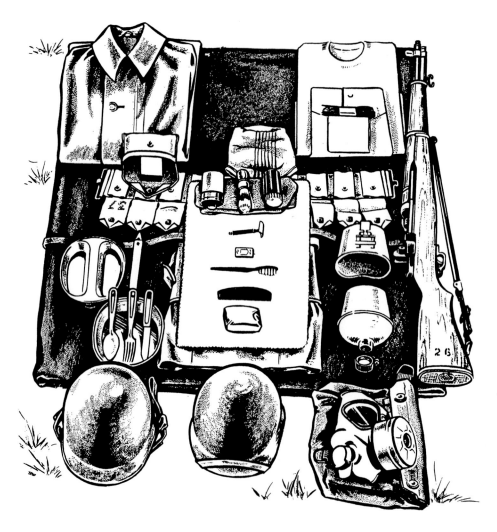

HELMET (OR LINER ONLY) MAY BE WORN DURING INSPECTION,
AS DIRECTED

APPENDIX II

Weight of the Soldier's Fighting Load

Based on clothing and equipment of a private first class rifleman (MOS 11B10) under non-winter conditions within a temperate zone climate, such as western Europe or the United States, during 1965.

Fighting Load Item	Weight in pounds	
A. Clothing		
M1 steel helmet assembly	3.44	
Leather combat boots	4.00	
Utility trousers and shirt	2.56	
Lightweight poncho	2.57	
Underwear and socks	.63	
Waist belt with buckle	.20	
Helmet camouflage band	.03	
Identification tags with necklace	.03	
Total	13.46	
B. Weapons		
Rifle: M16 (M14)	6.90	(9.08)
Ammunition: 180 rounds M16 (100 rounds M14)	6.21	(7.85)
Smoke grenades x 2	3.00	
Fragmentation grenades x 2	2.00	
Bayonet with scabbard	1.30	
Total, armed with M16 (M14)	19.41	(23.23)

C. Equipment

Sleeping bag w/carrier, pneumatic mattress	12.96
Intrenching tool and carrier	4.00
Canteen (filled) with cup and cover	3.60
M17 ABC field protective mask w/carrier	2.97
Field pack w/2 pairs of underwear, socks	1.89
Individual equipment belt with suspenders	1.52
Small arms ammunition case x 2	1.50
Rifle cleaning kit	.60
First aid dressing with case	.44
Total	29.48

D. Rations

Combat meal (to be placed in field pack)	1.77
Mess kit with fork, knife, and spoon	.56
Water purification tablets and bottle	.06
Total	2.39

Total weight, armed with M16 (M14 rifle)	64.74	(68.56)

GLOSSARY

AAA: *Antiaircraft artillery*
ABC: *Army biological-chemical*
Abn: *Airborne*
AF: *Air Force*
AG: *Adjutant General*
Armd: *Armored*
AWOL: *Absent without leave*
Bde: *Brigade*
Bn: *Battalion*
Cav: *Cavalry*
CBR: *Chemical-biological-radiological*
Class A: *The highest level of locally prescribed uniform classification, which generally mandated a coat or jacket with shirt and necktie for winter and a shirt with necktie for summer wear. This was the normal uniform classification for leaving the post and for special occasions.*
Class B: *The uniform classification that generally mandated that a necktie was not required. This was the uniform usually worn during normal duty hours.*
CG: *Commanding General*
COFS: *Chief of Staff*
CONARC: *Continental Army Command*
CW: *Chemical warfare*
DA: *Department of the Army*

DI: *Drill Instructor*
Div: *Division*
DMS: *Direct molded sole*
ERDL: *Engineer Research and Development Laboratory*
GCM: *Gold-colored metal (usually plain solid brass)*
HALO: *High Altitude, Low Opening*
HBT: *Herringbone twill*
Inf: *Infantry*
LINCLOE: *Lightweight Individual Clothing and Equipment Project*
M: *Model*
MOS: *Military Occupational Specialty*
MP: *Military Police*
MQ: *Model Quartermaster*
NCO: *Noncommissioned Officer*
OCS: *Officer Candidate School*
OD: *Olive drab*
OG: *Olive green*
PASGT: *Personnel Armament System Ground Troops*
QMCTC: *Quartermaster Corps Technical Committee*
SCARWAF: *Special Category Army with Air Force (phased out in 1957). These were primarily engineer and specialist units*

engaged in air base construction and repair.

STABO: *Designation derived from harness developers Stevens, Knabb, and Roberts (see author's* U.S. Army Uniforms of the Vietnam War, *p. 149.)*

SWB: *Special Warfare Board*

T: *Type, also Test*

TDA: *Table of Distribution and Allowances*

TW: *Tropical worsted*

UNC: *United Nations Command*

USMA: *United States Military Academy*

WAC: *Women's Army Corps*

WOC: *Warrant Officer Candidate*

Index